Bible

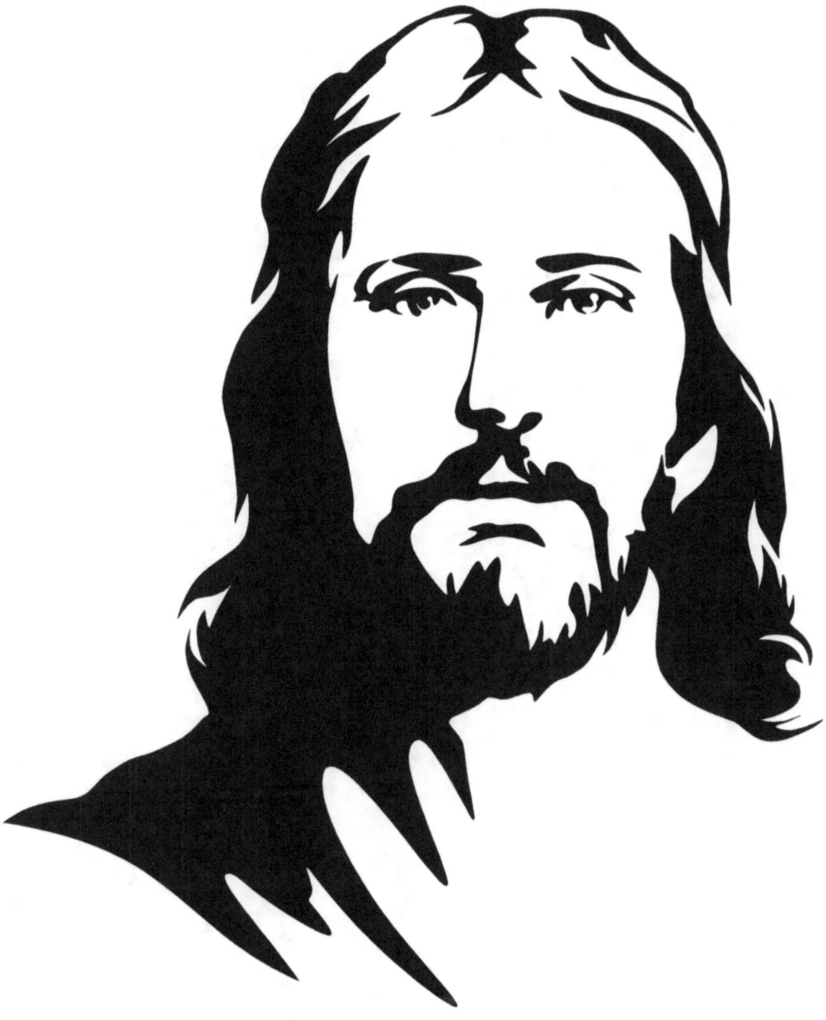

Coloring book

Test color

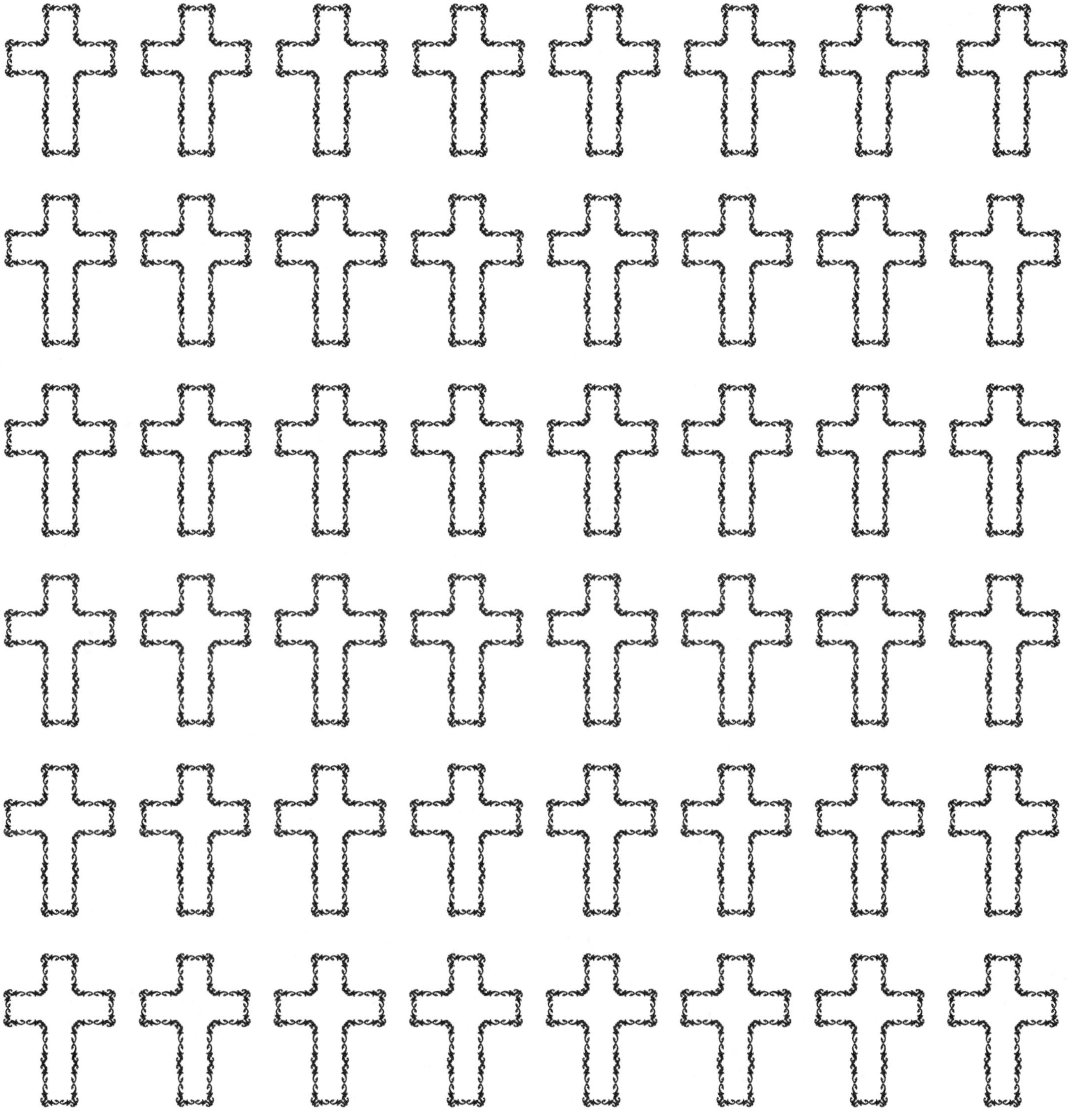

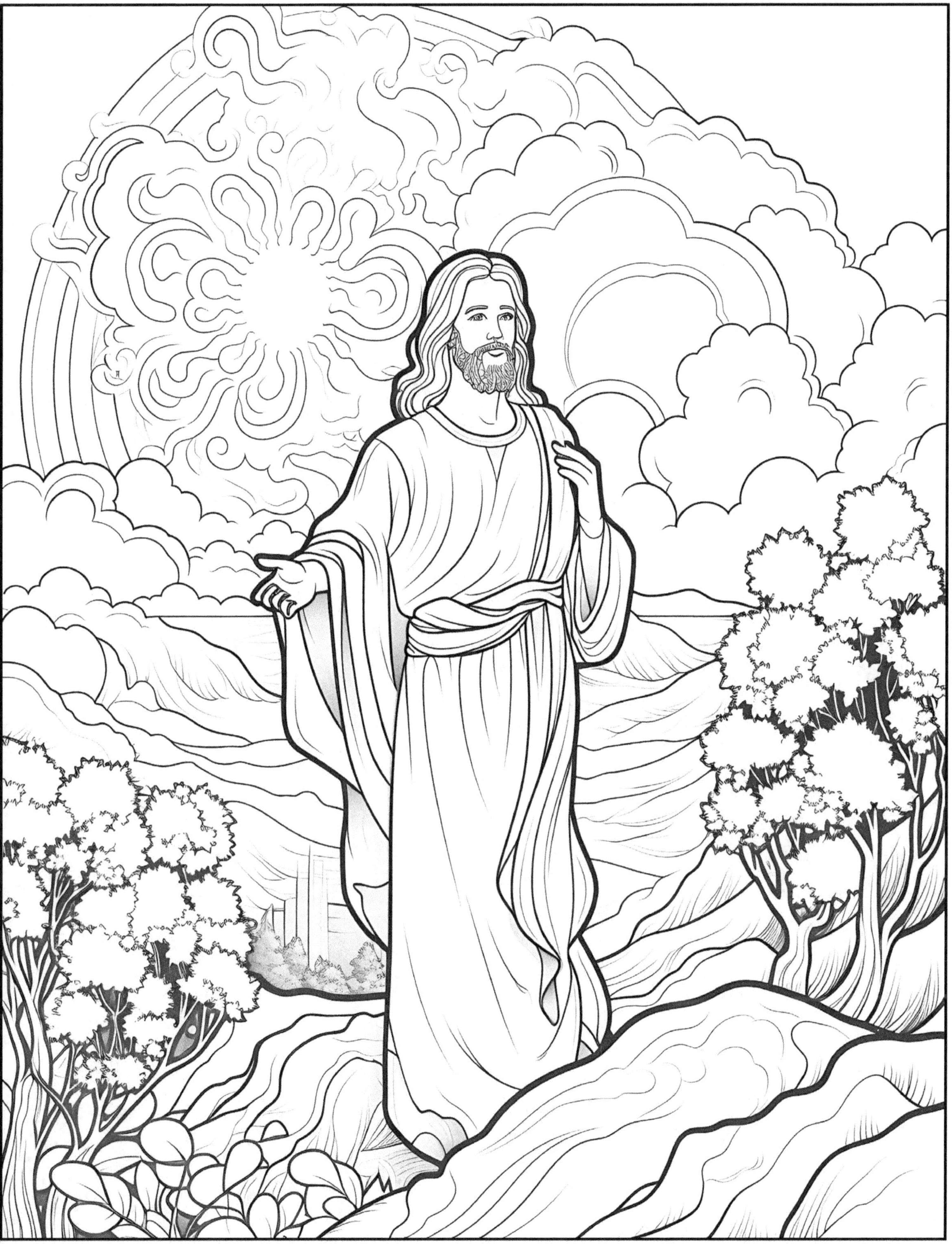

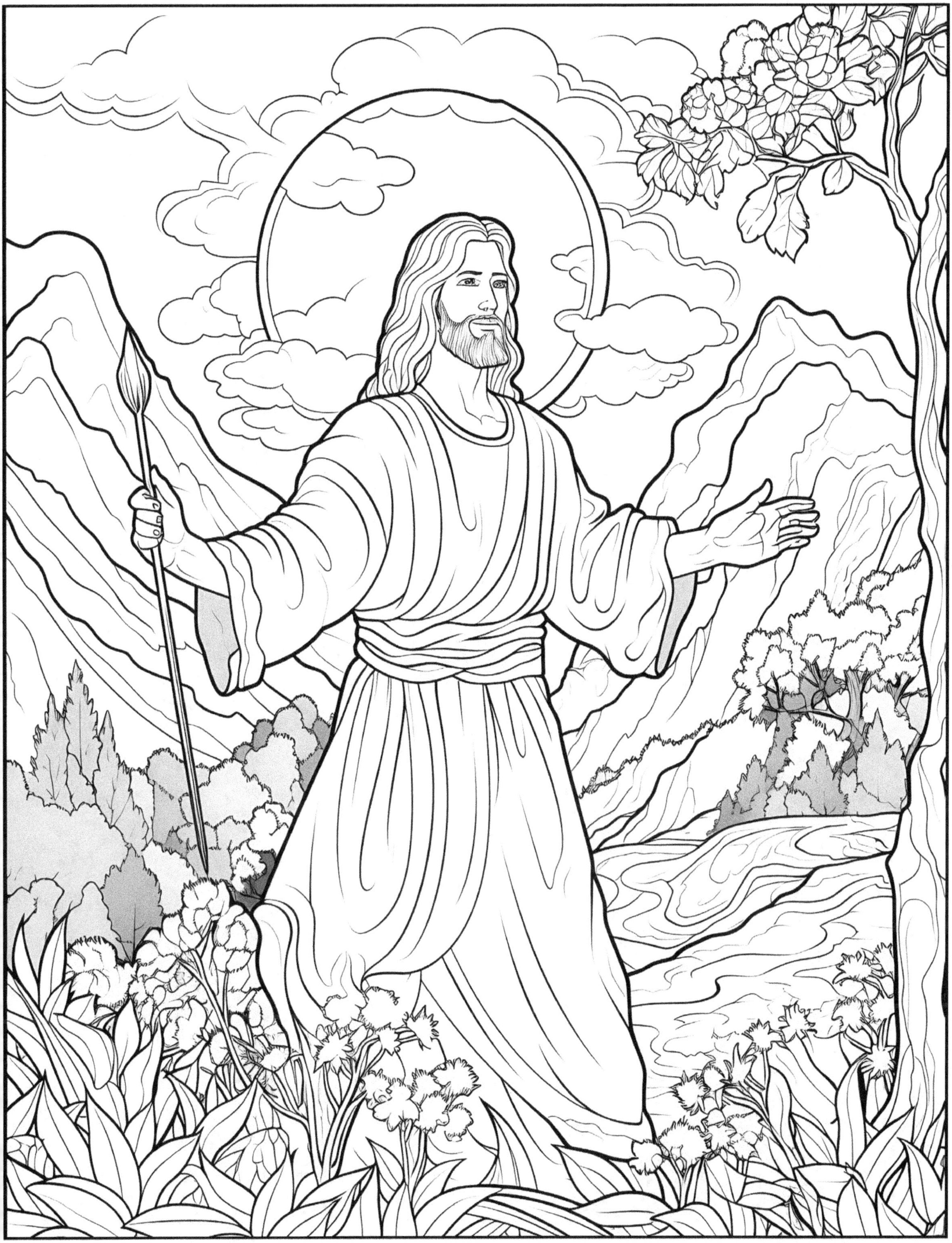

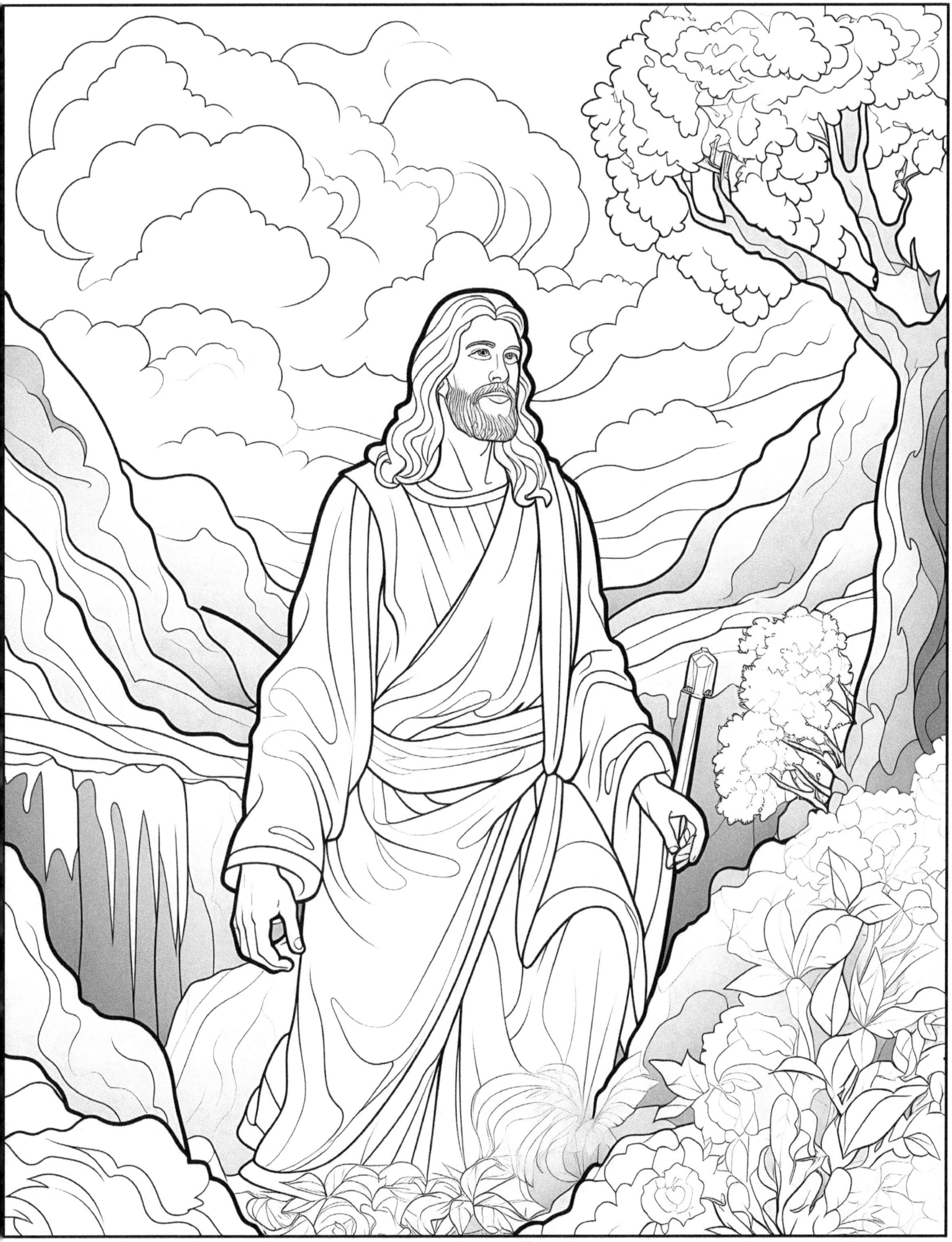

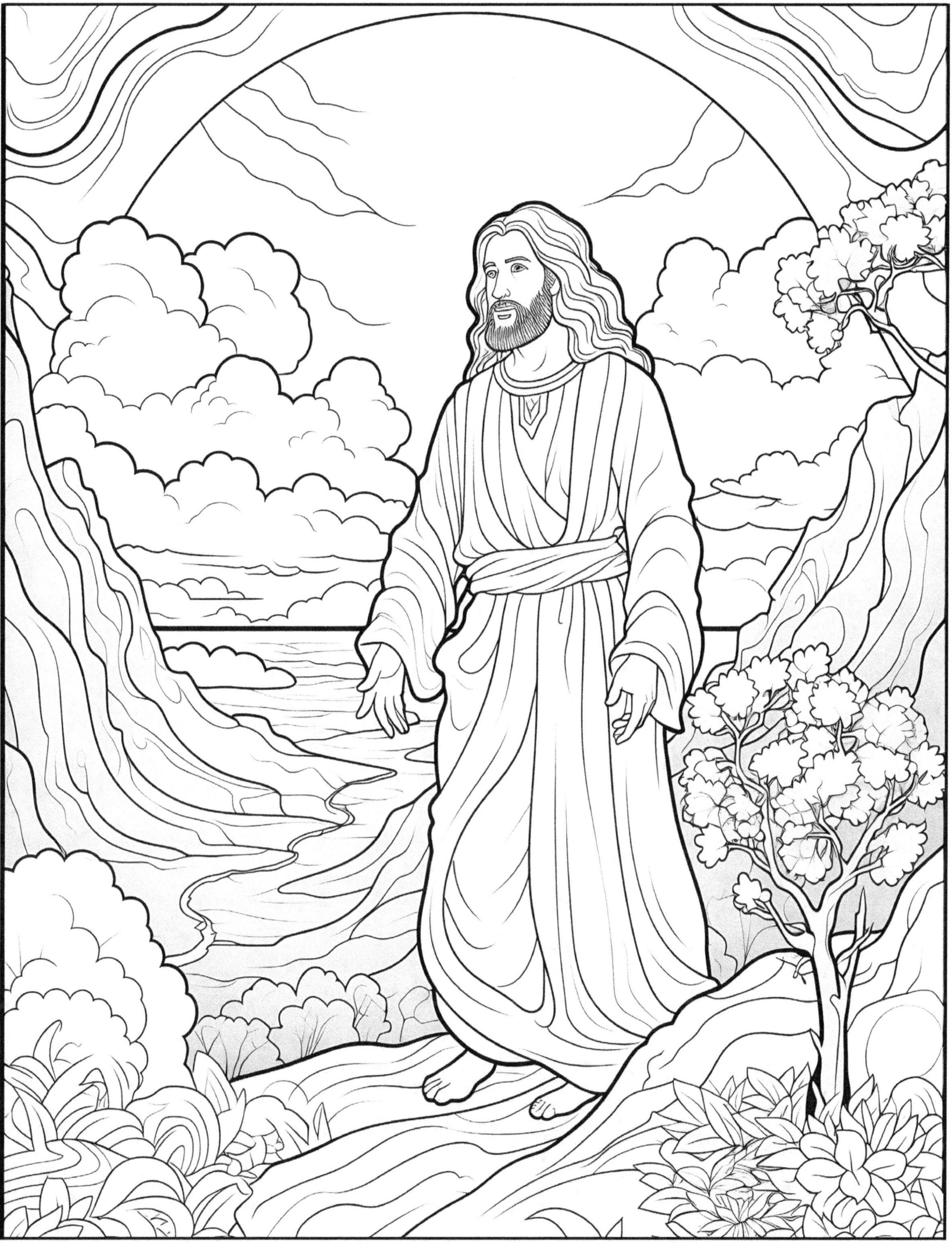

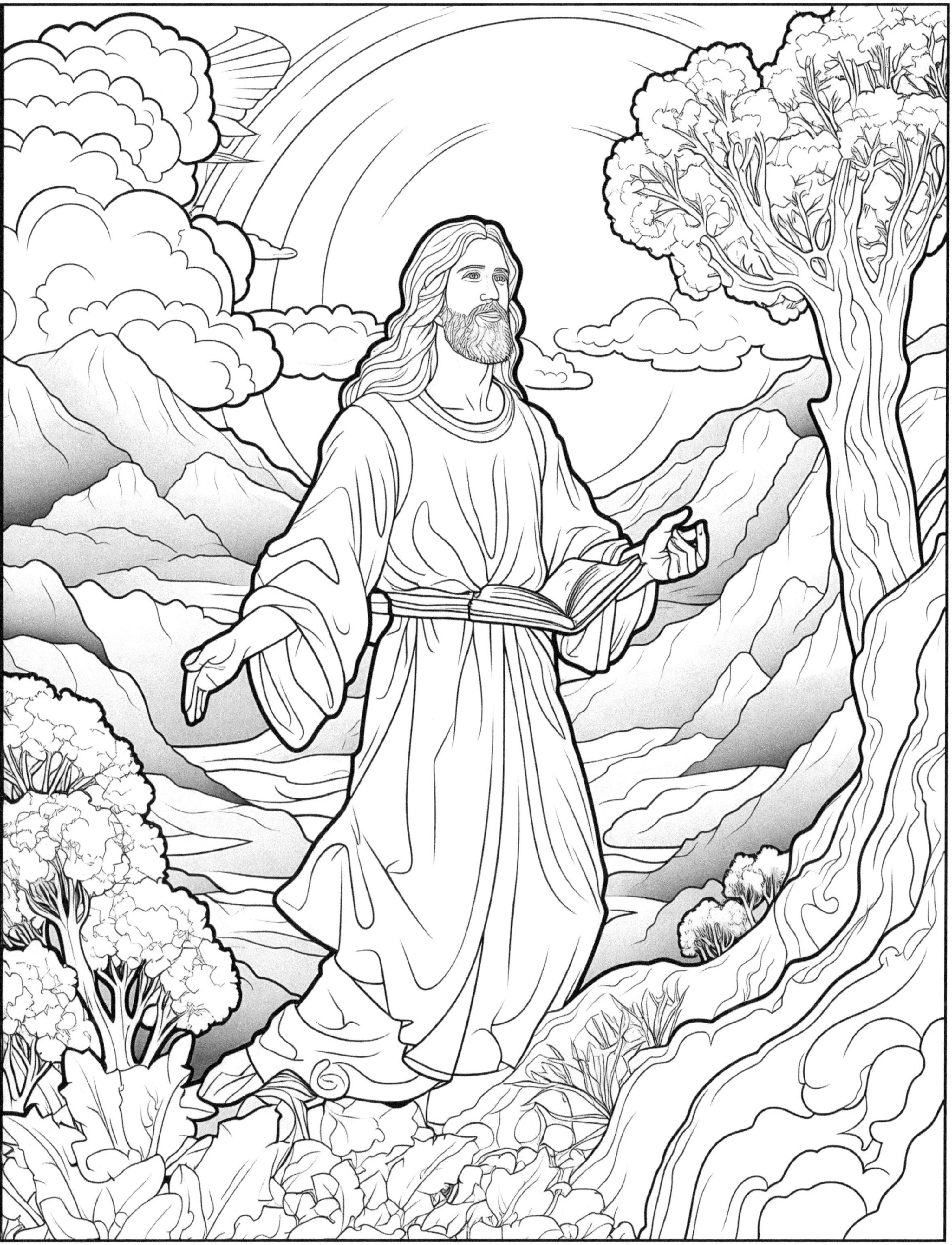

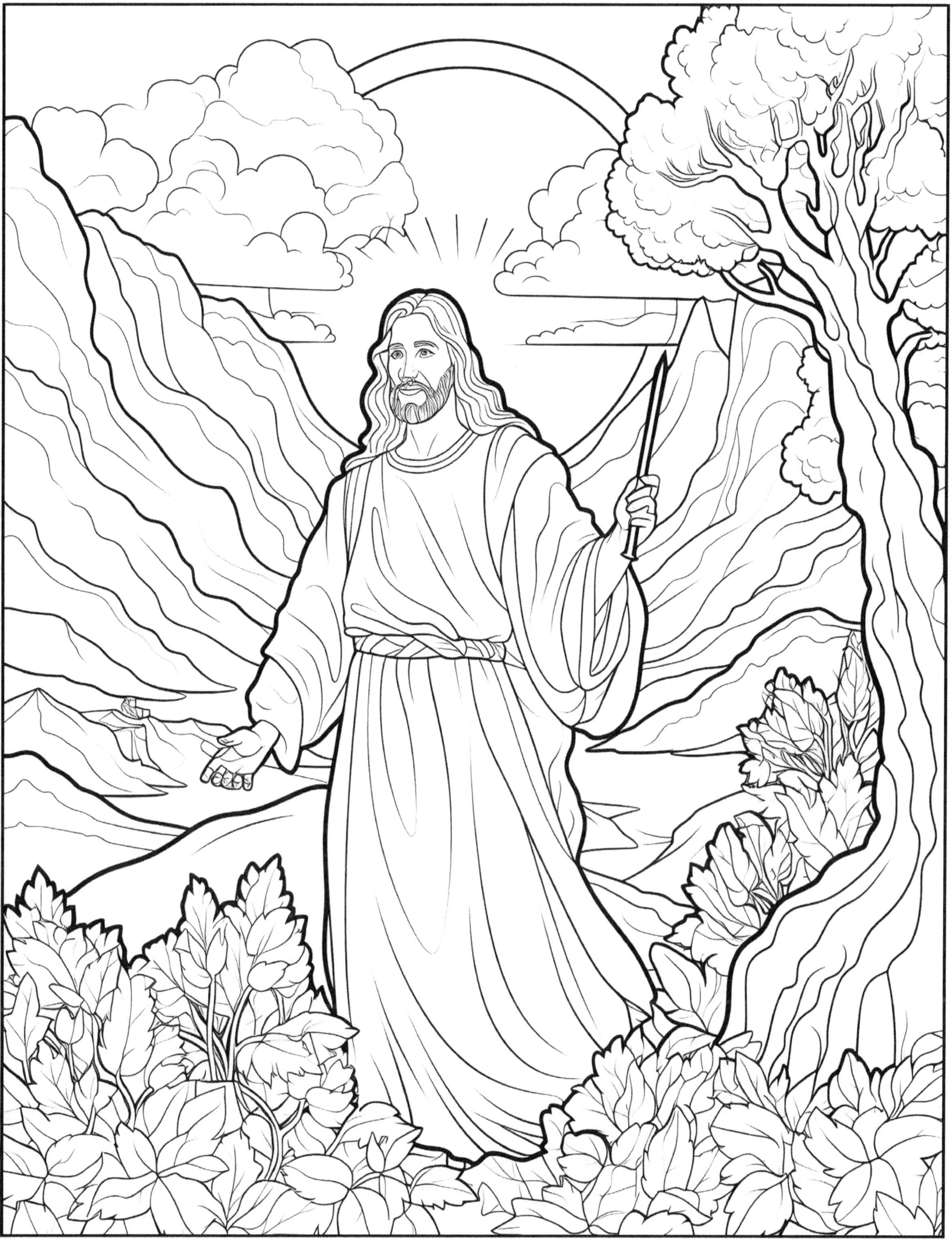

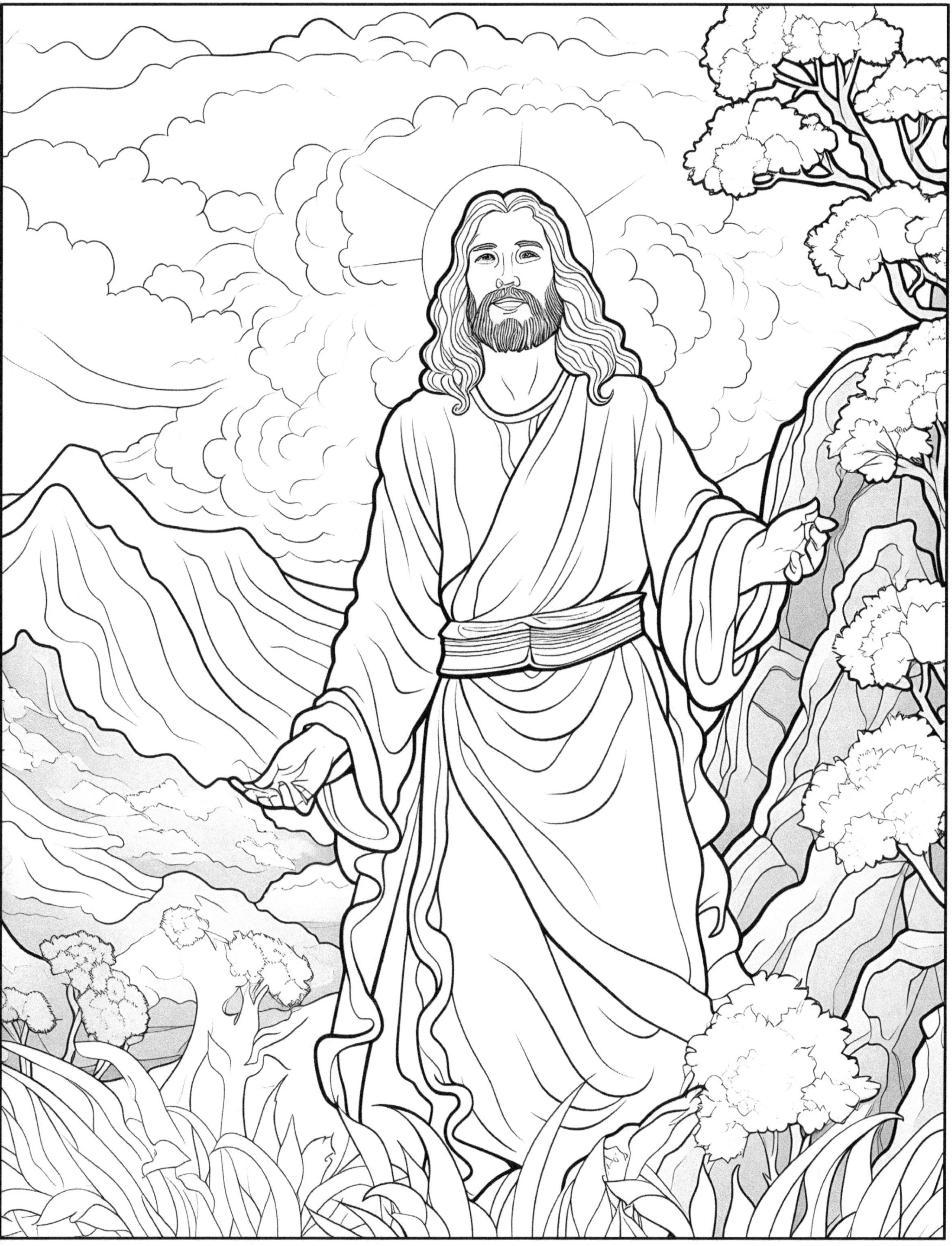

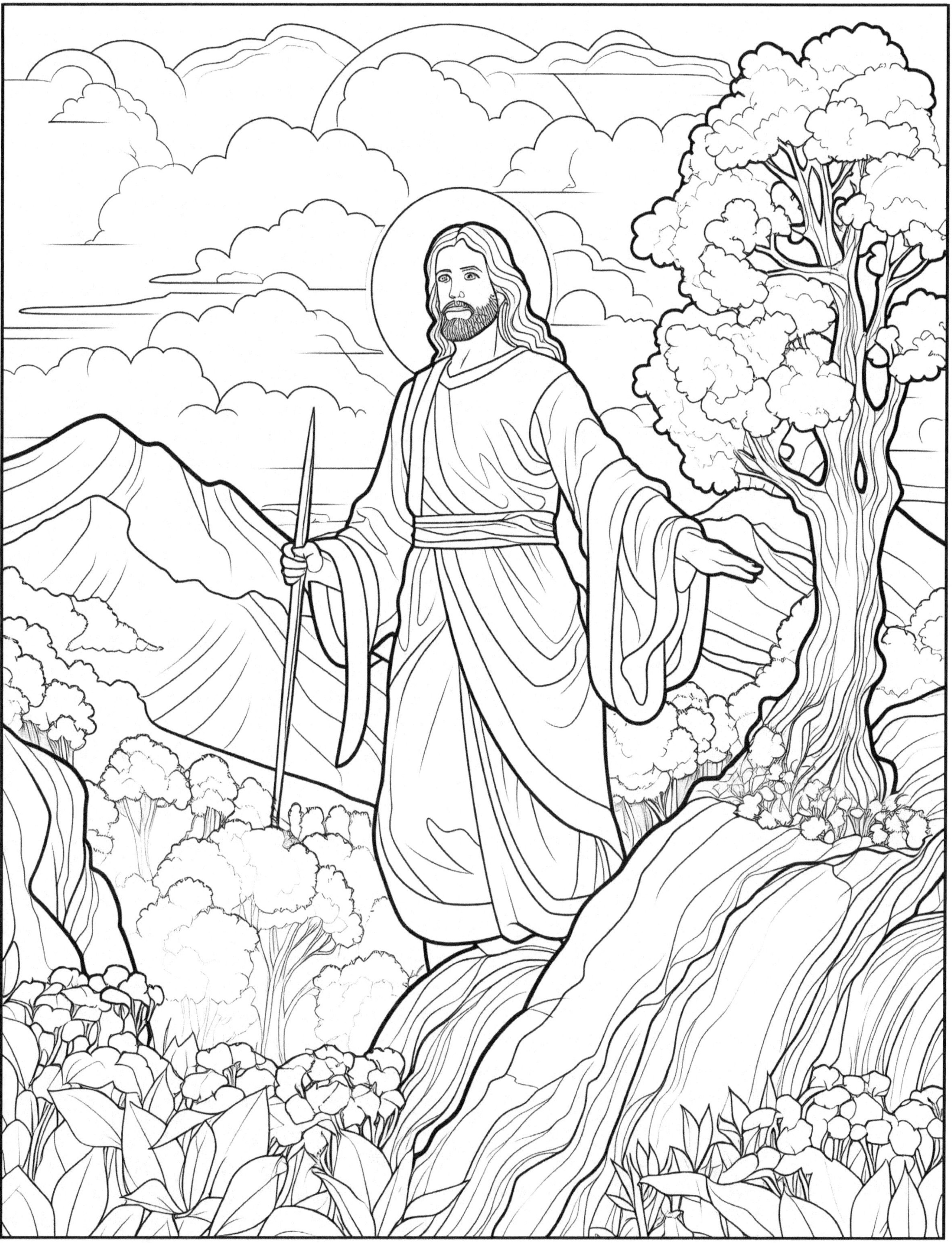

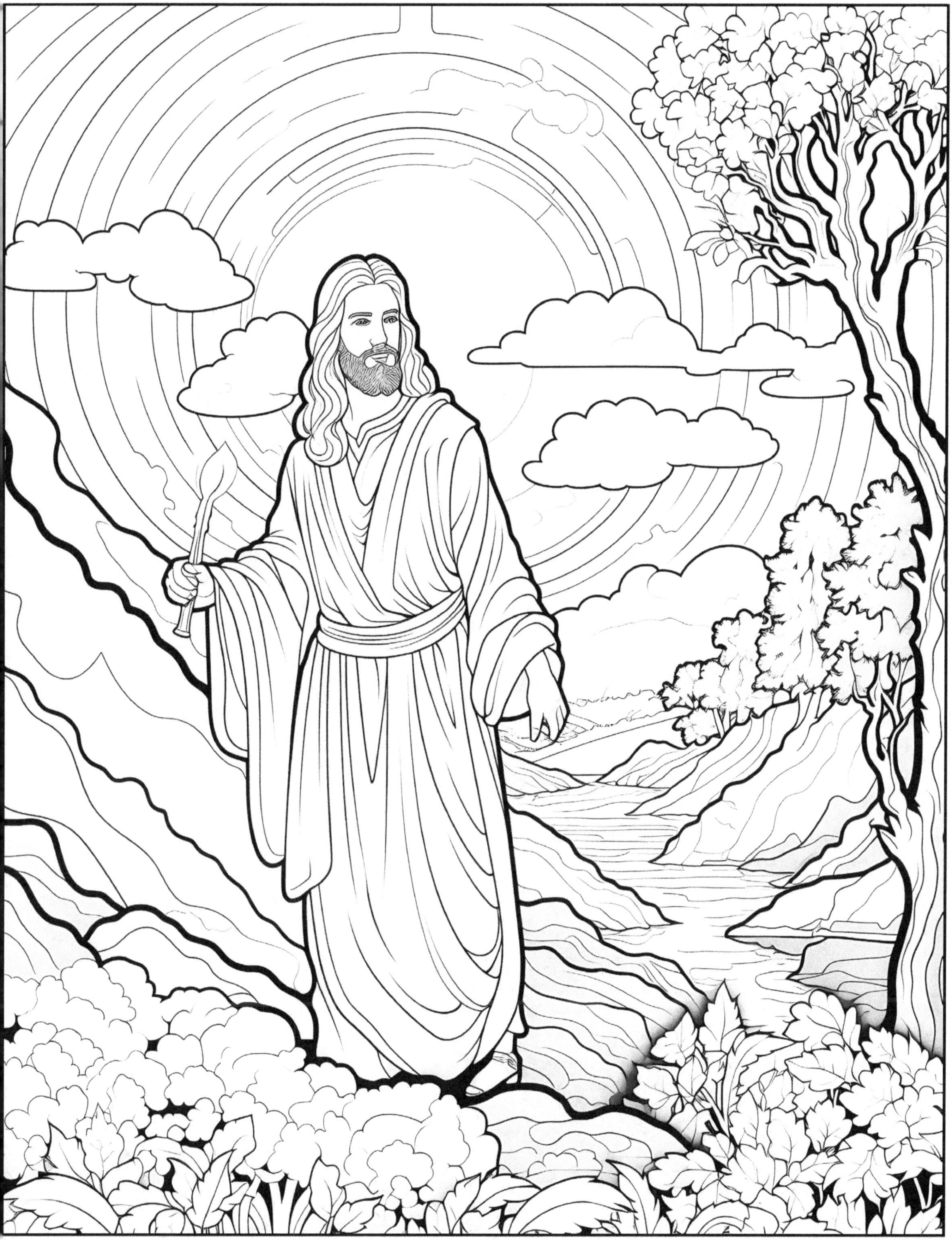

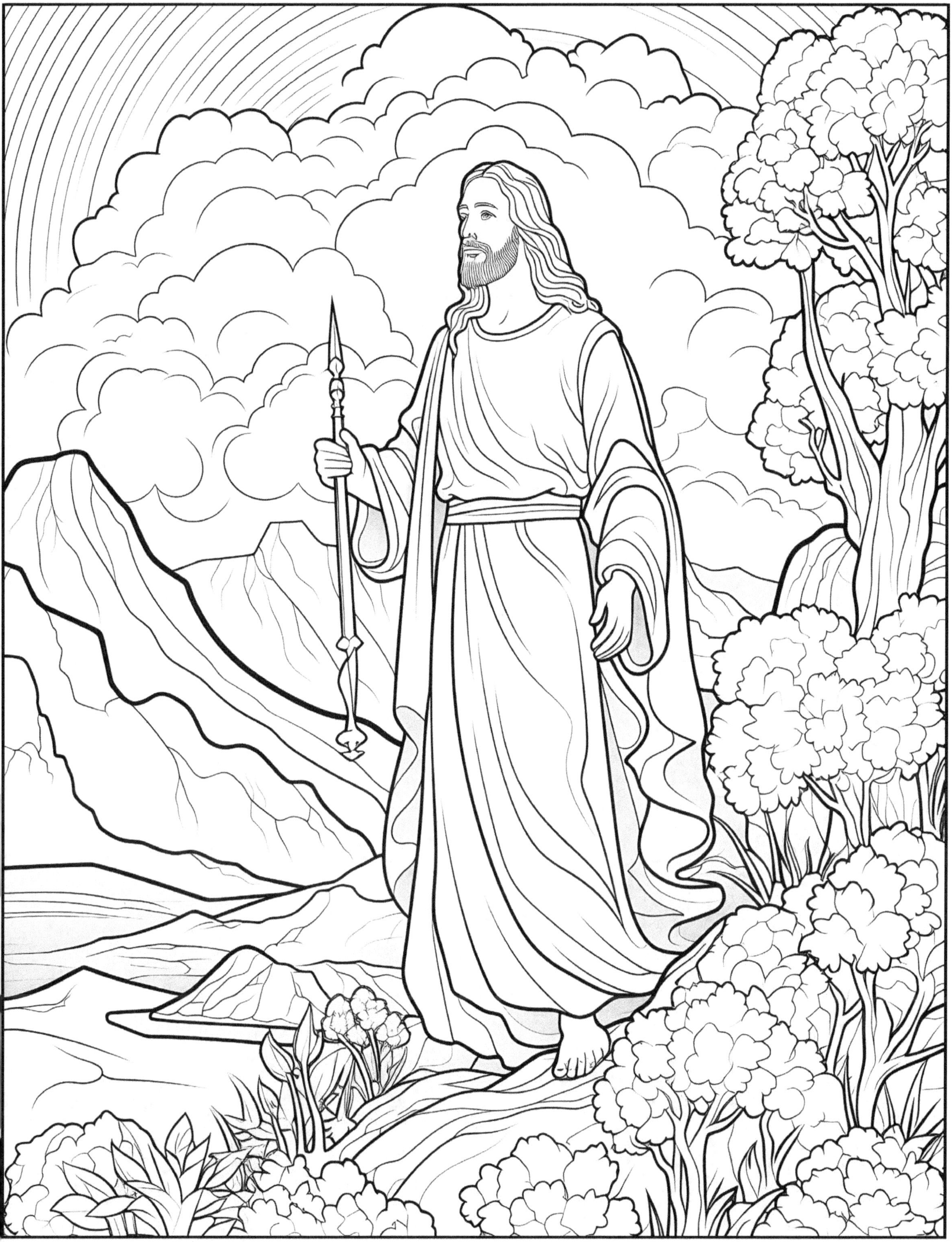

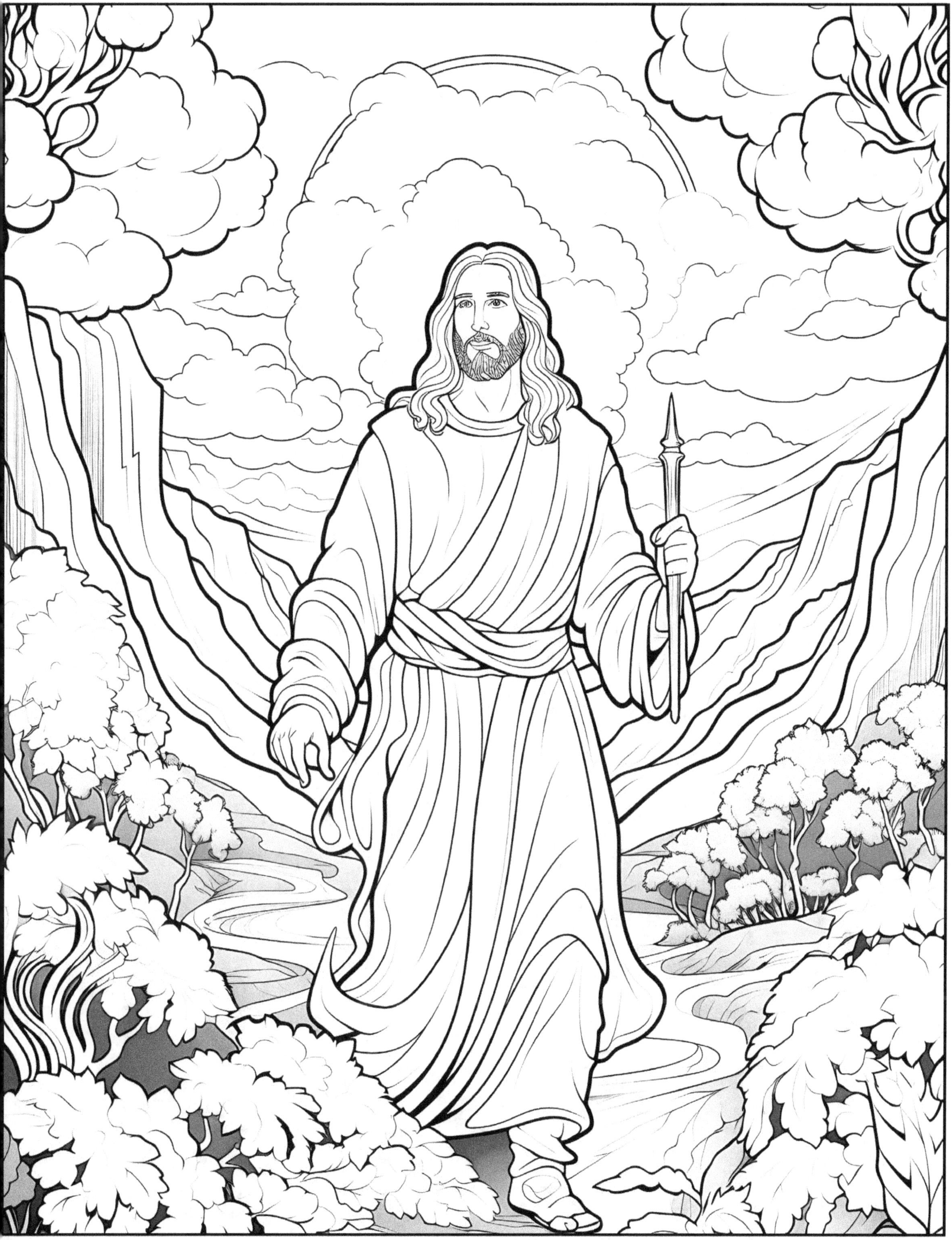

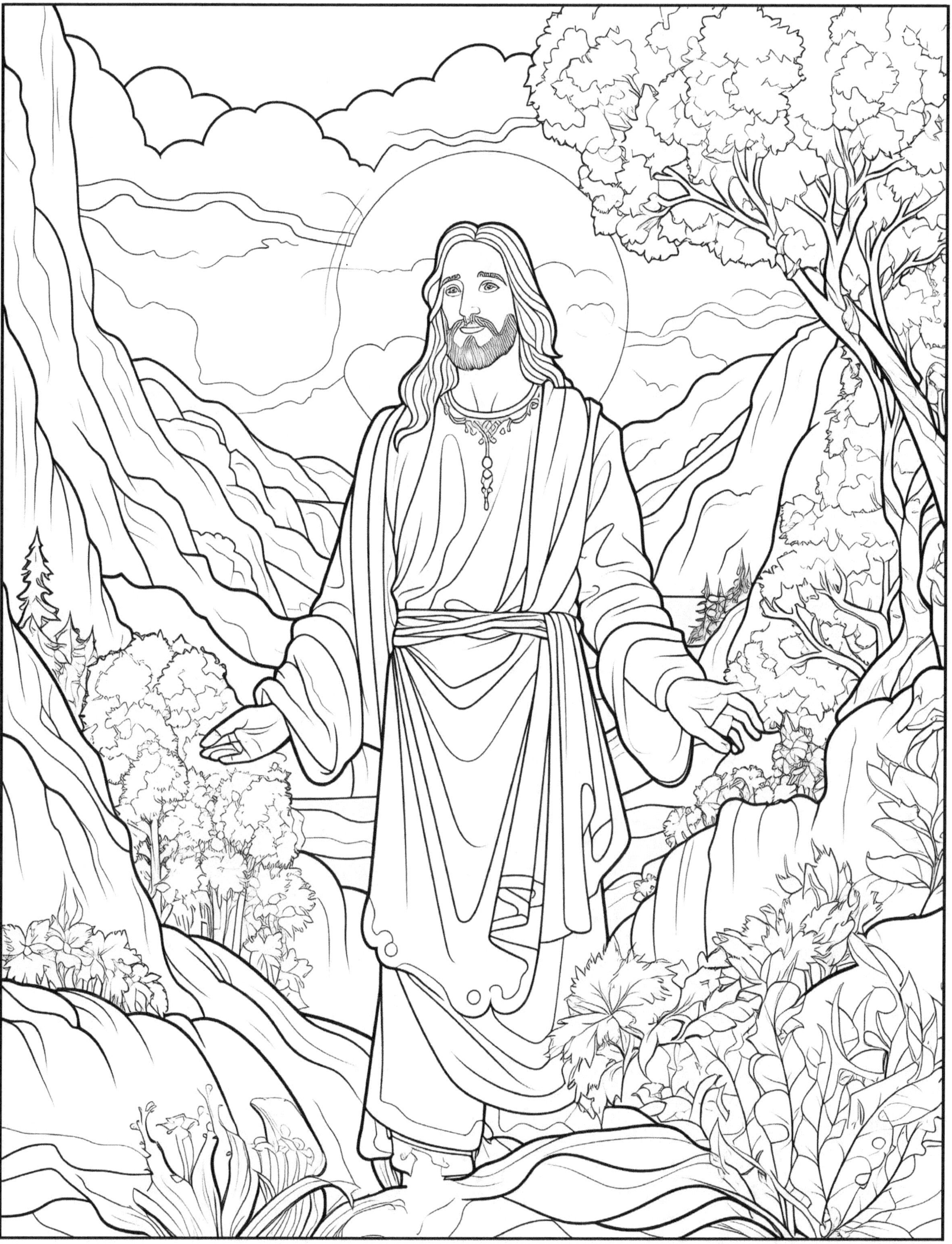

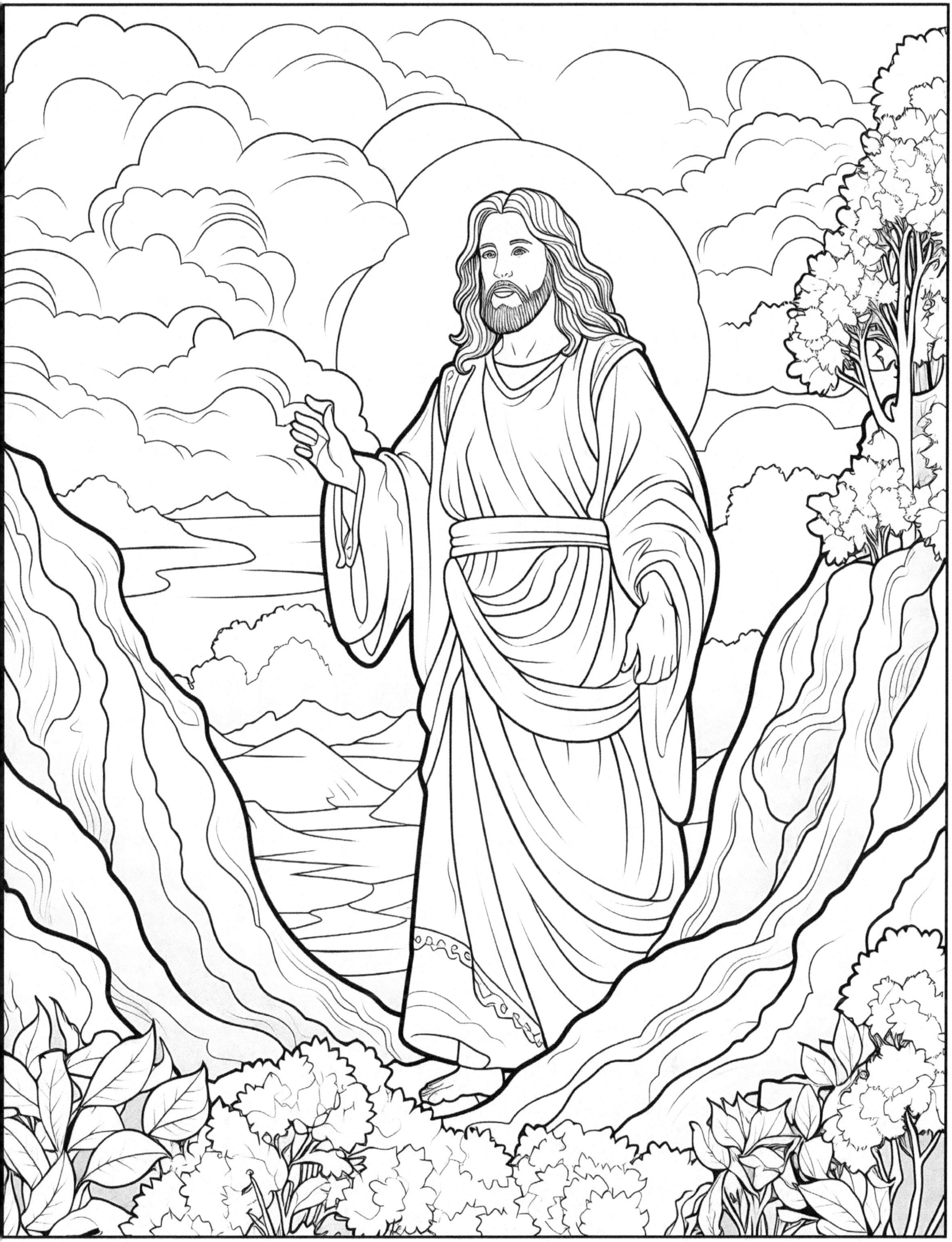

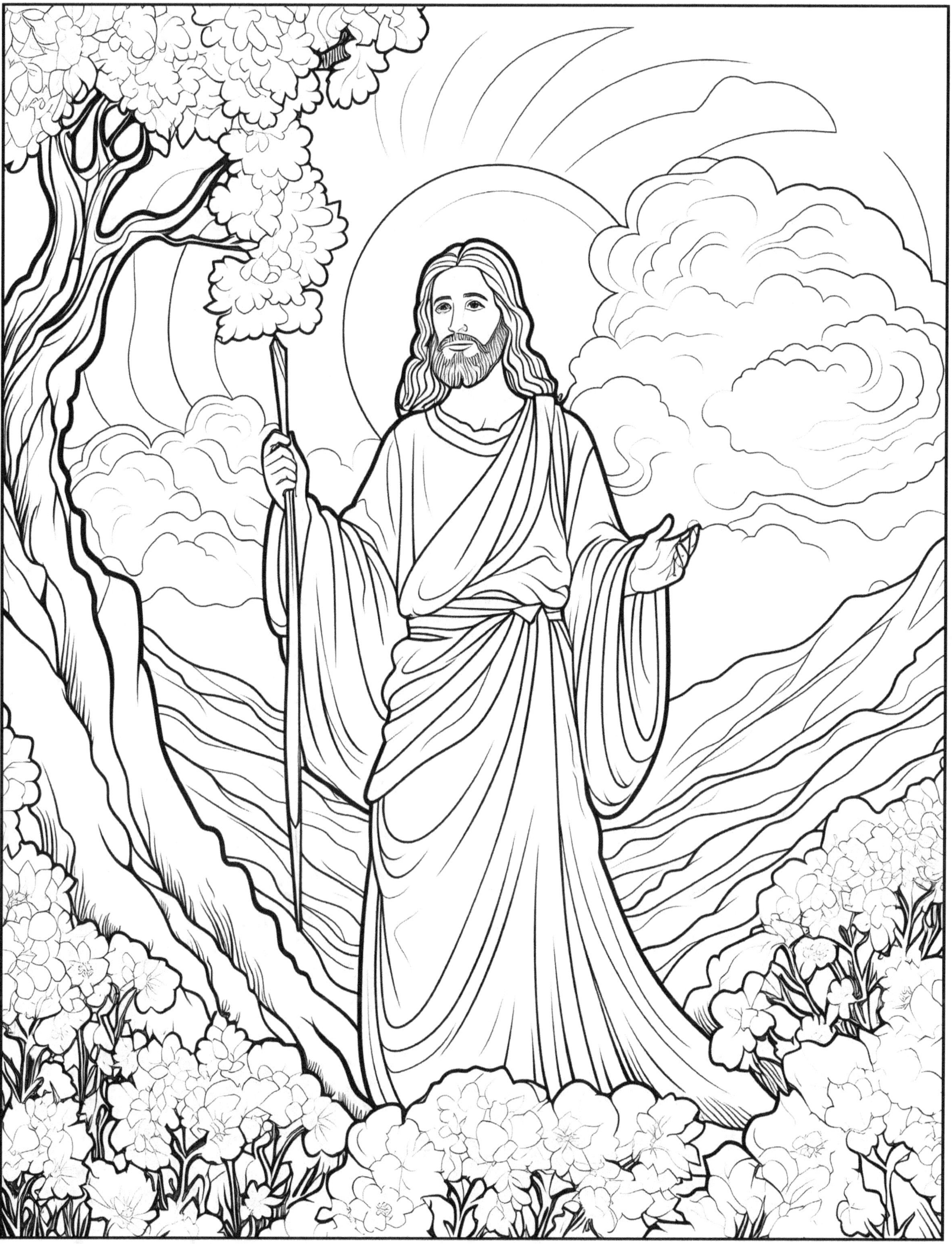

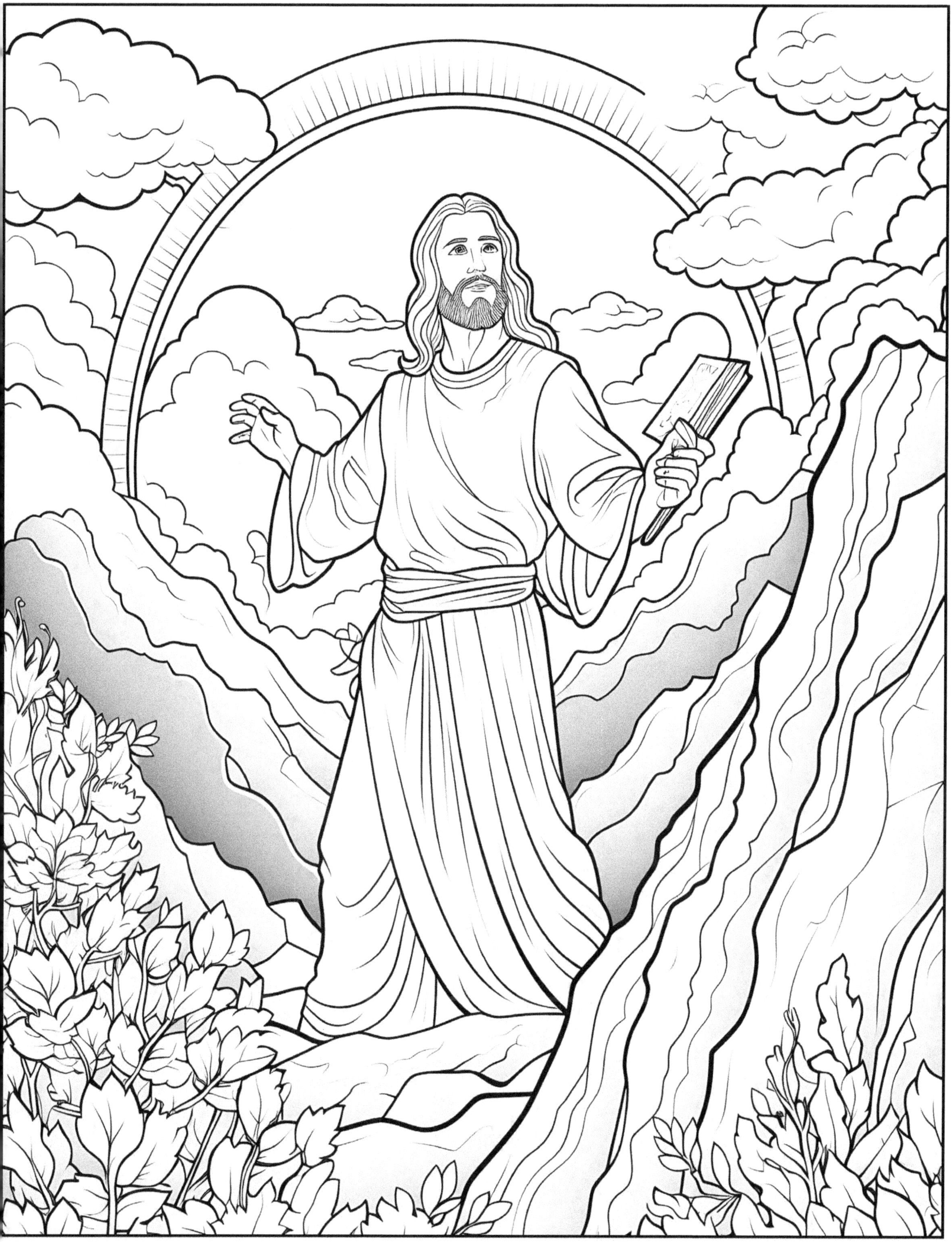

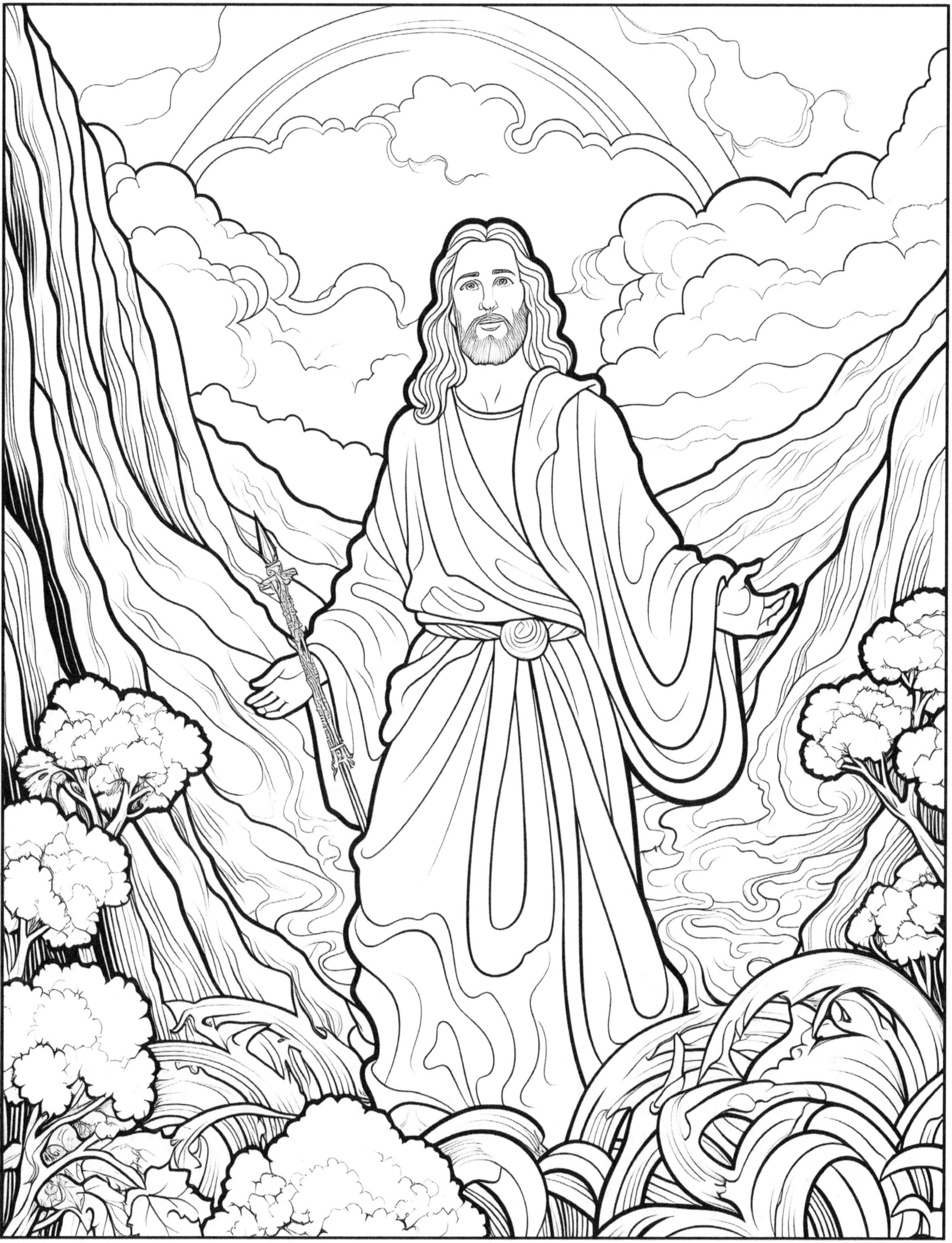

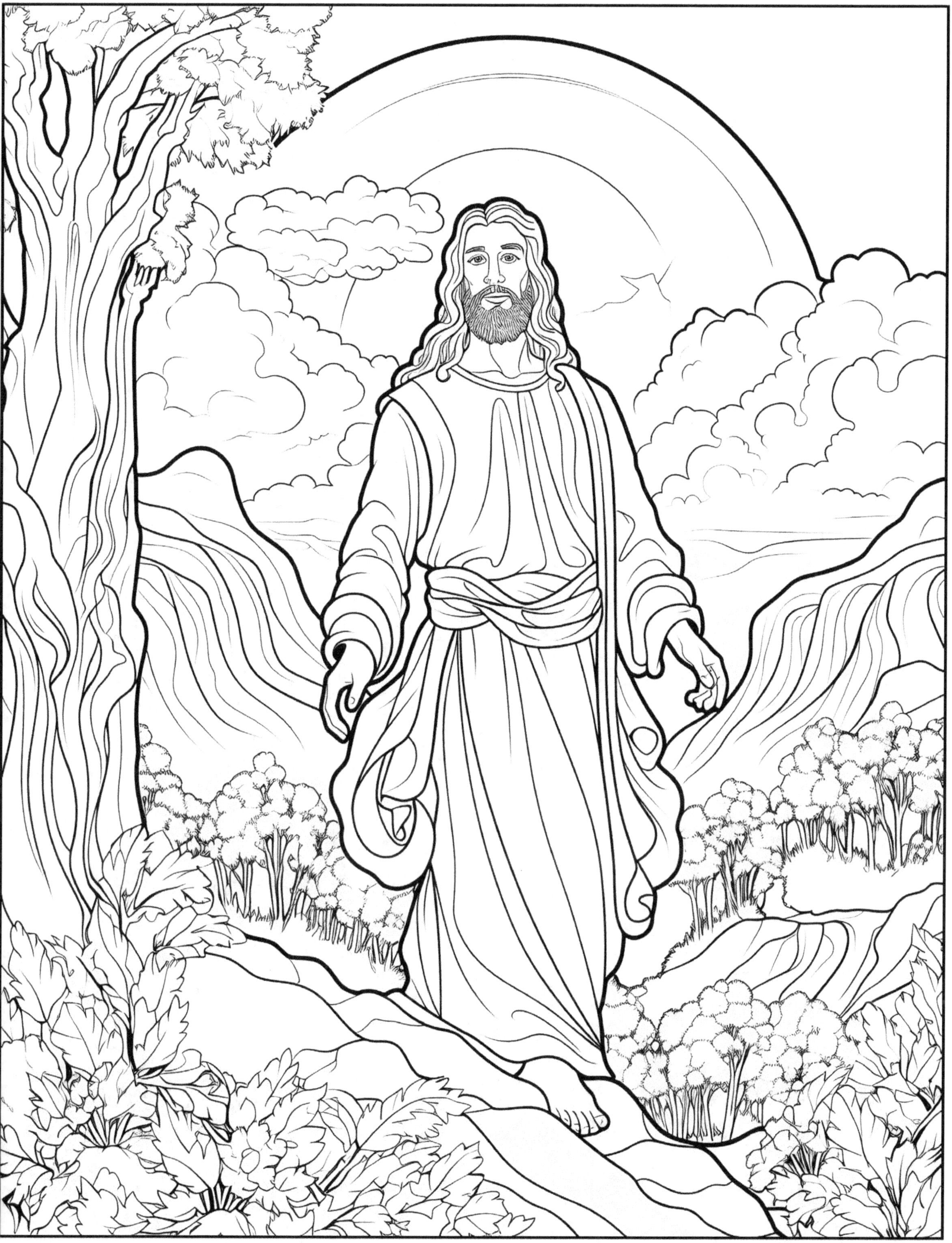

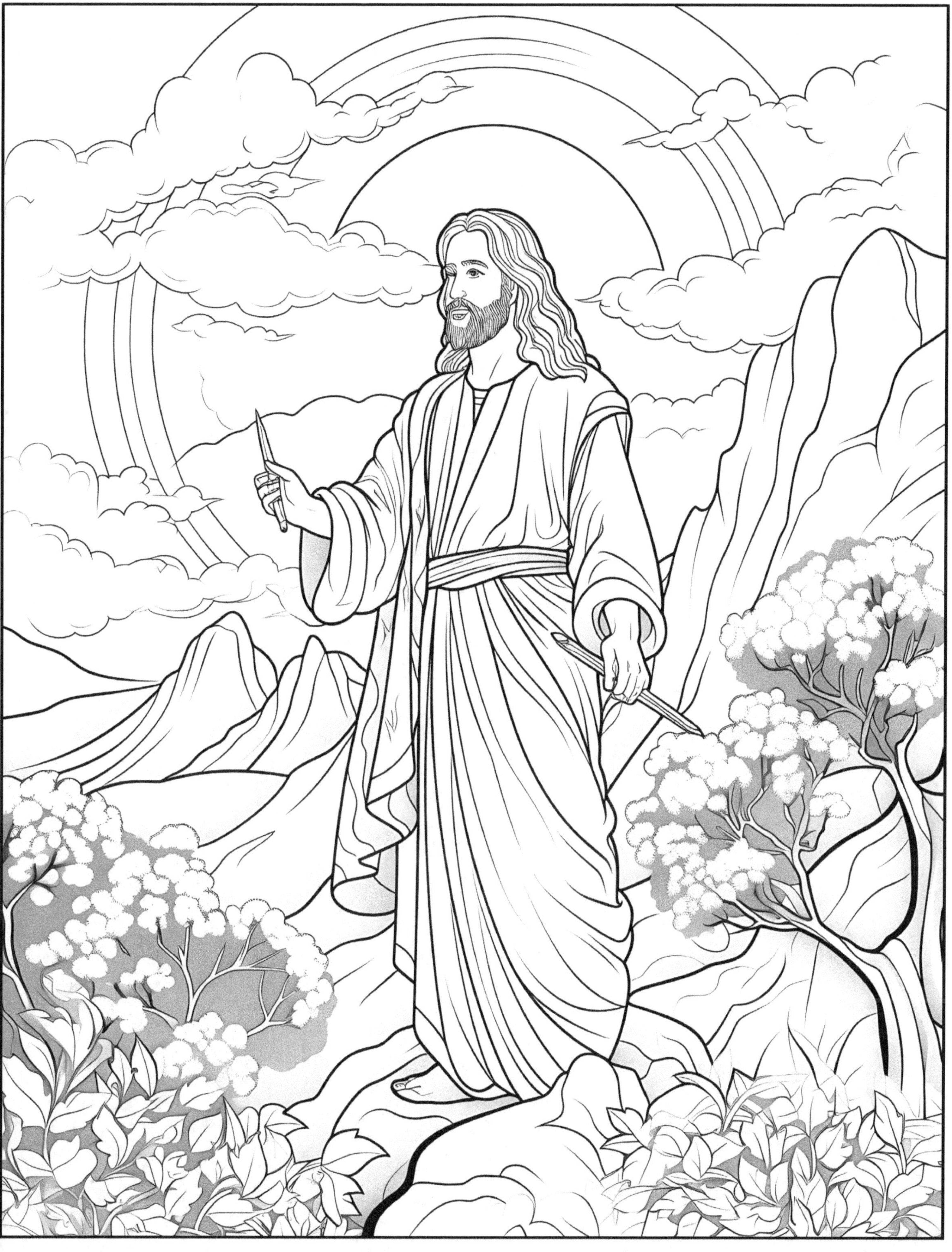

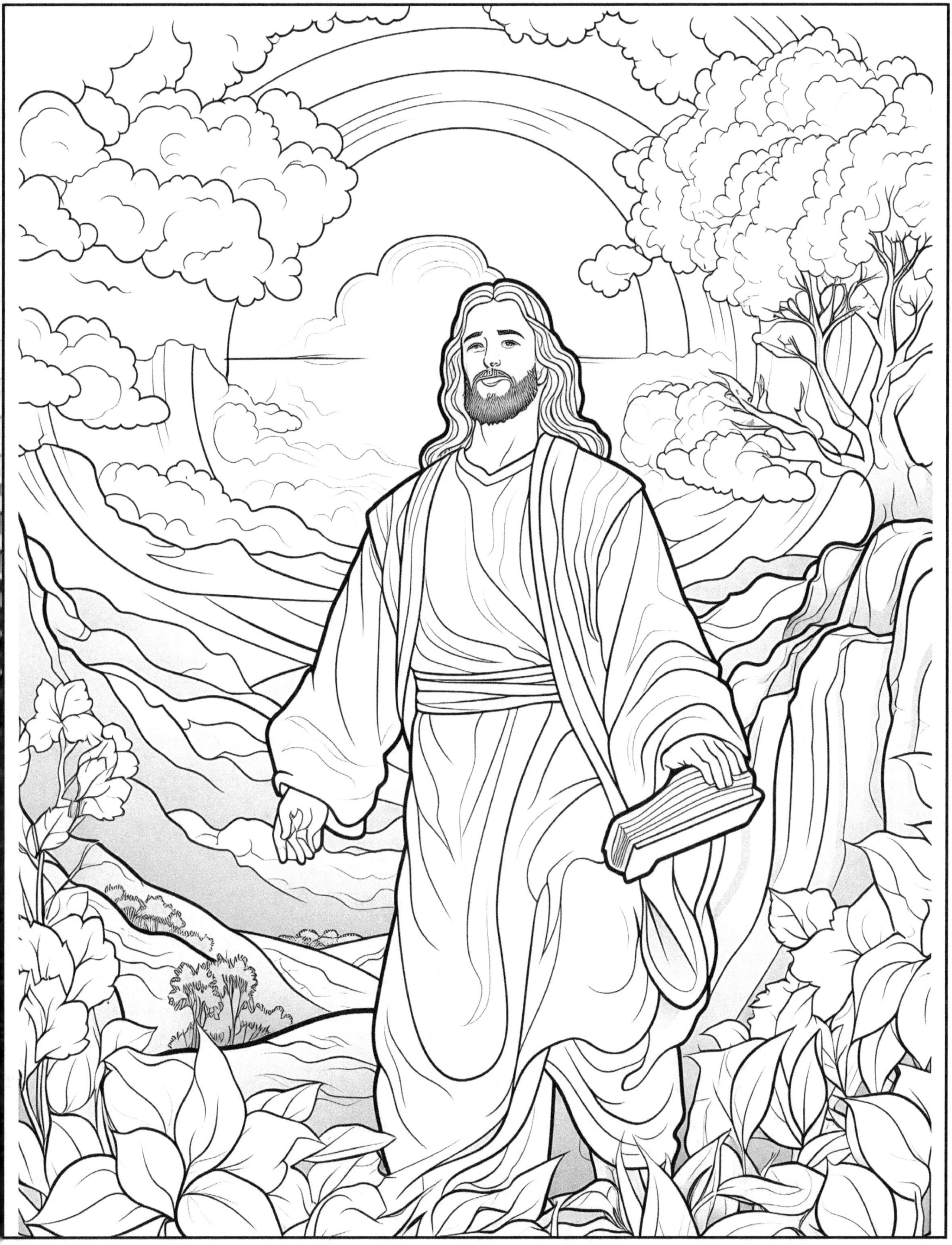

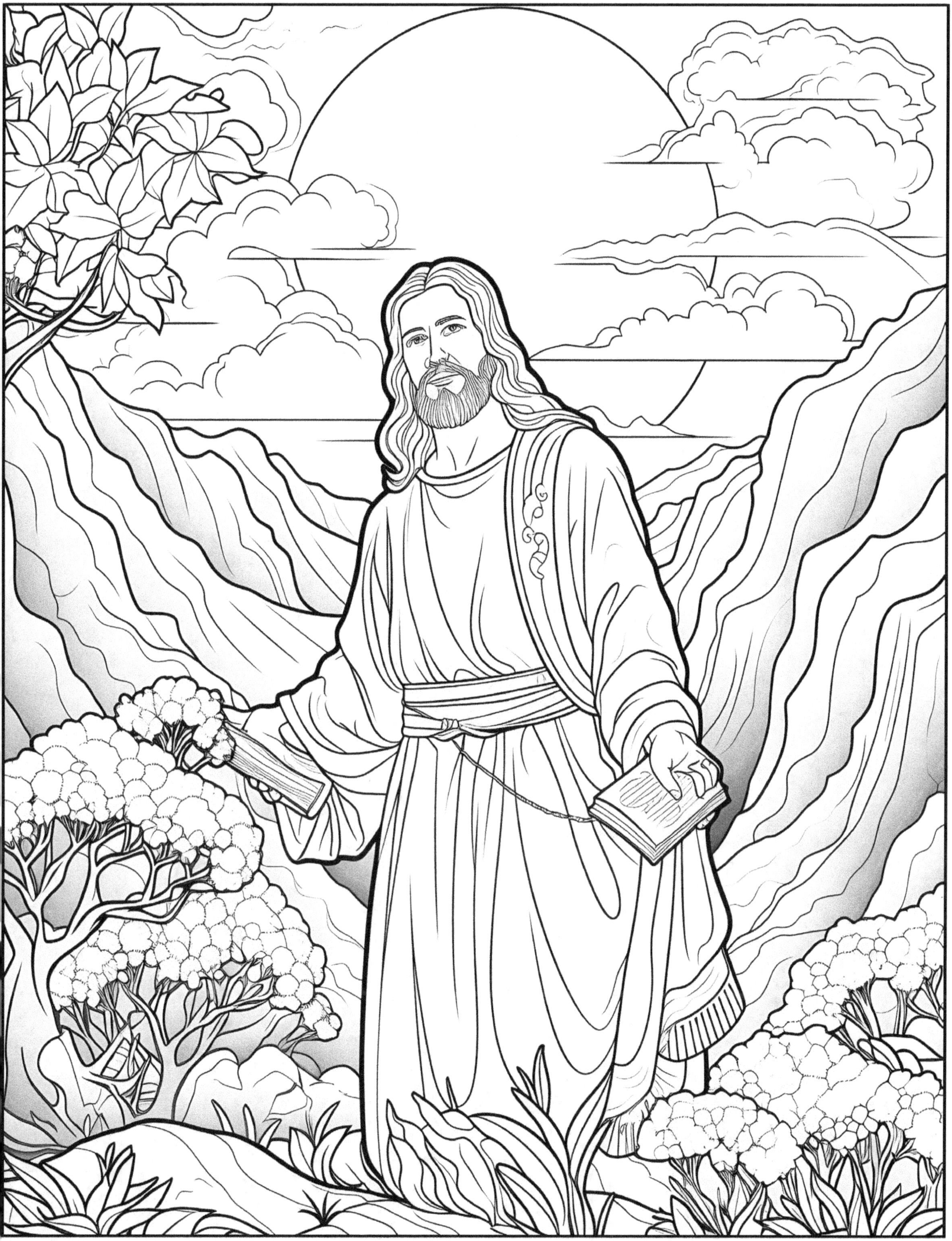

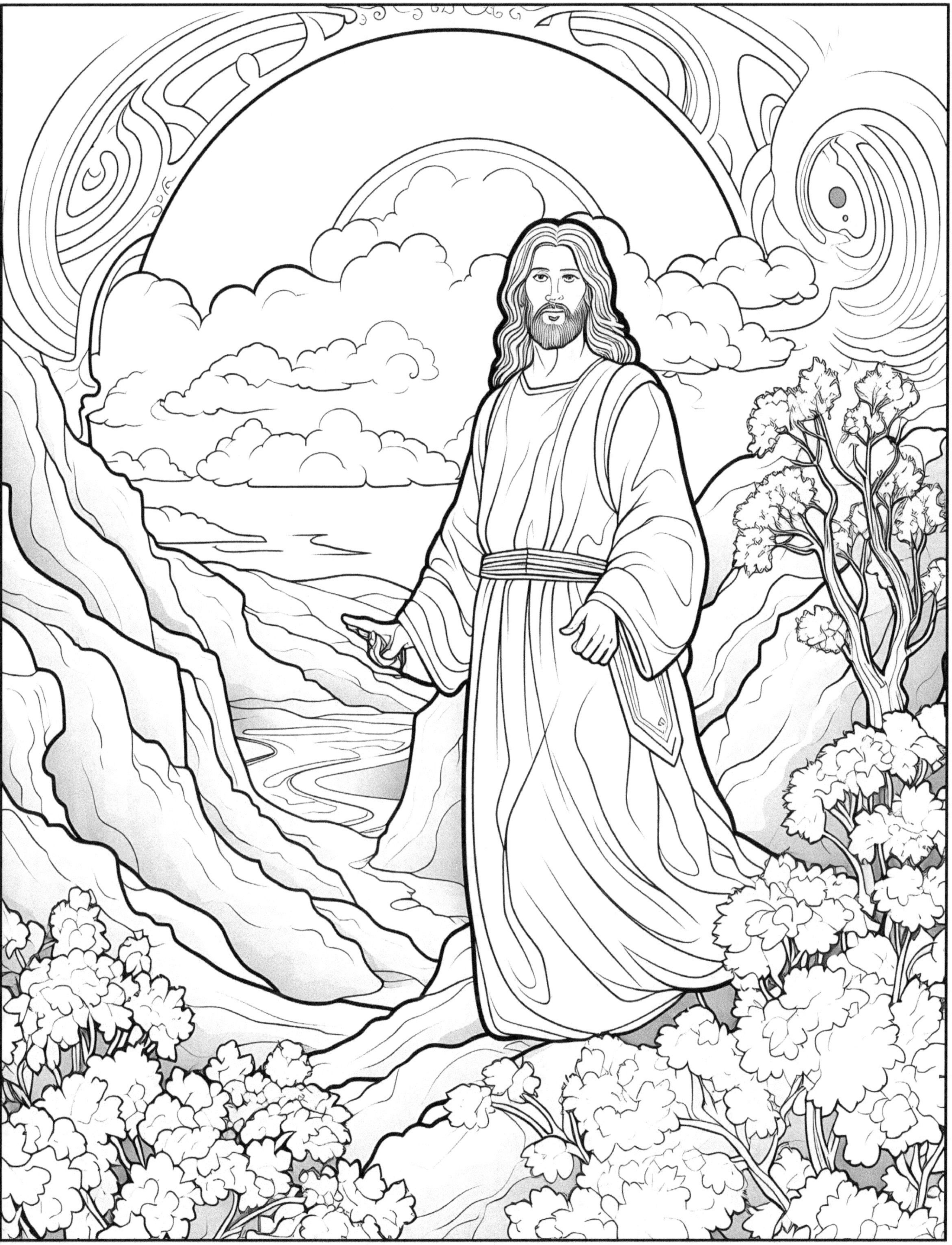

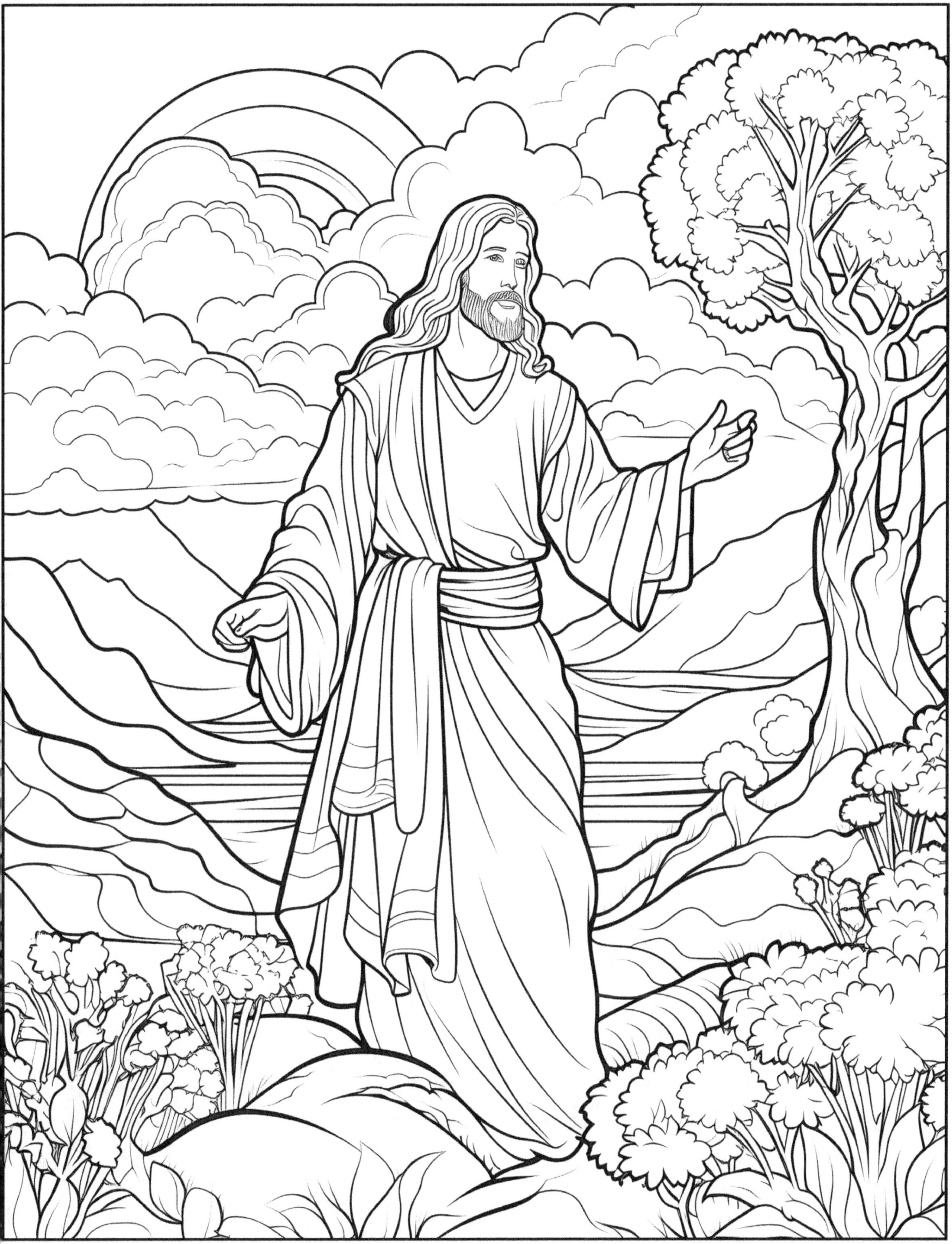

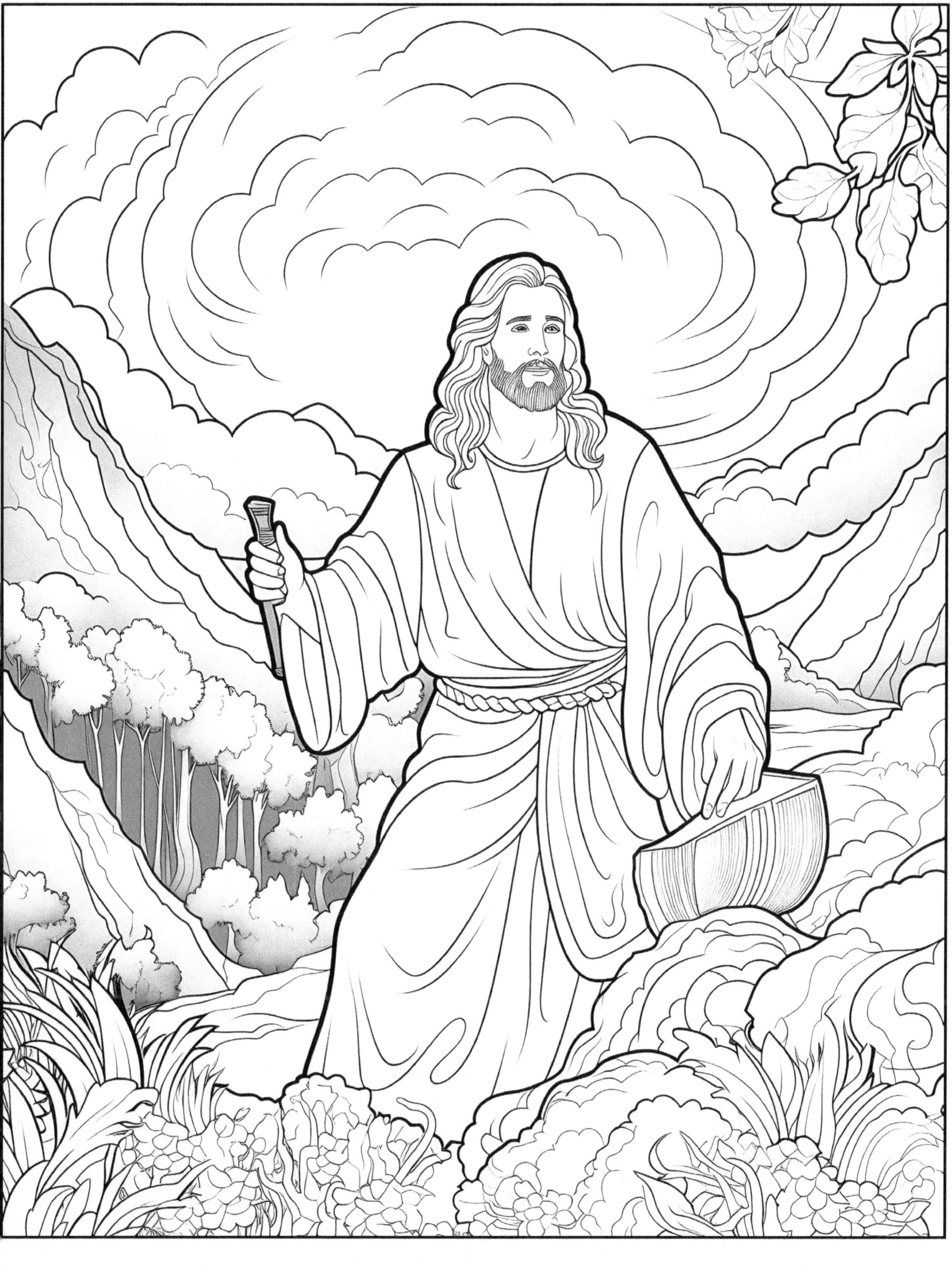

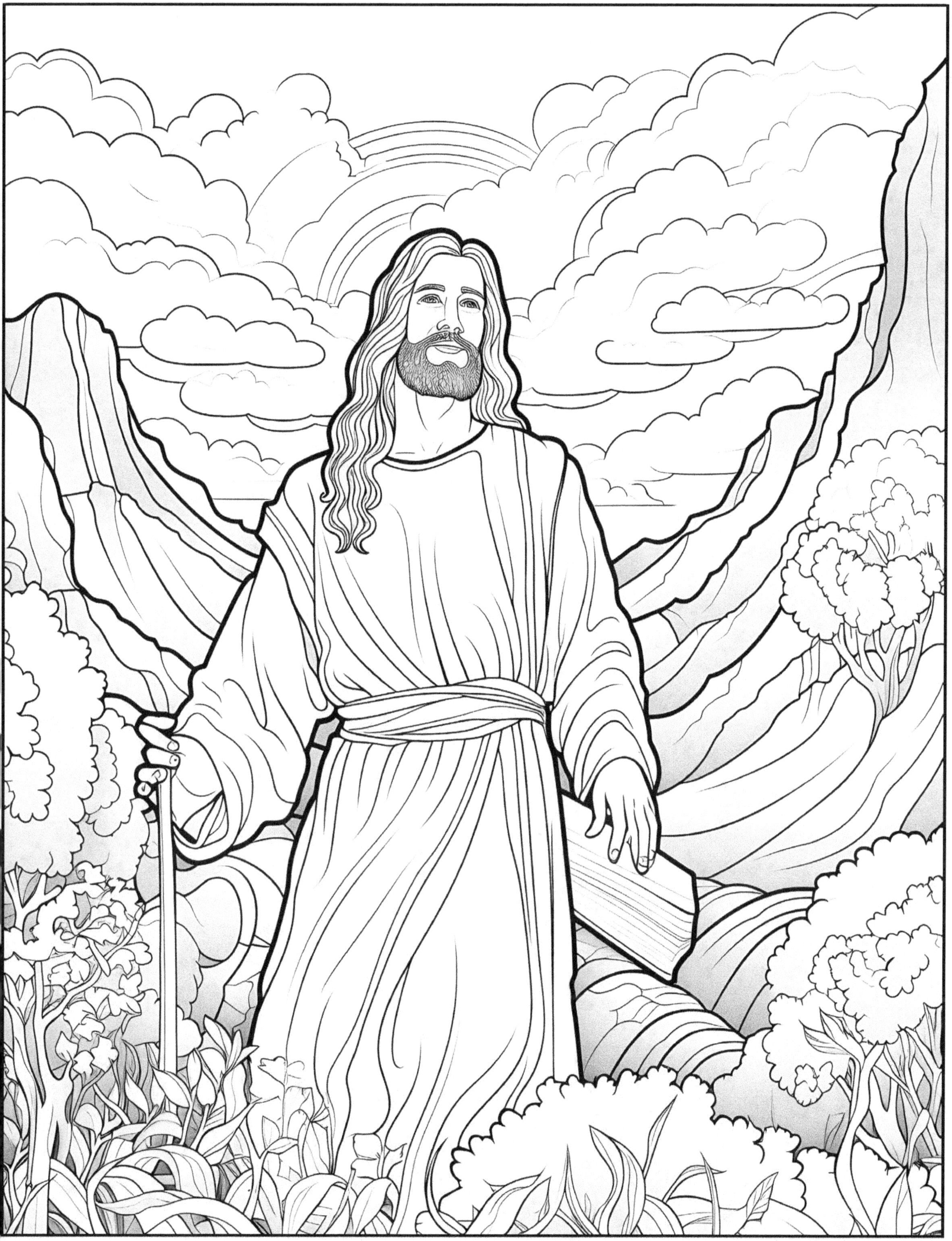

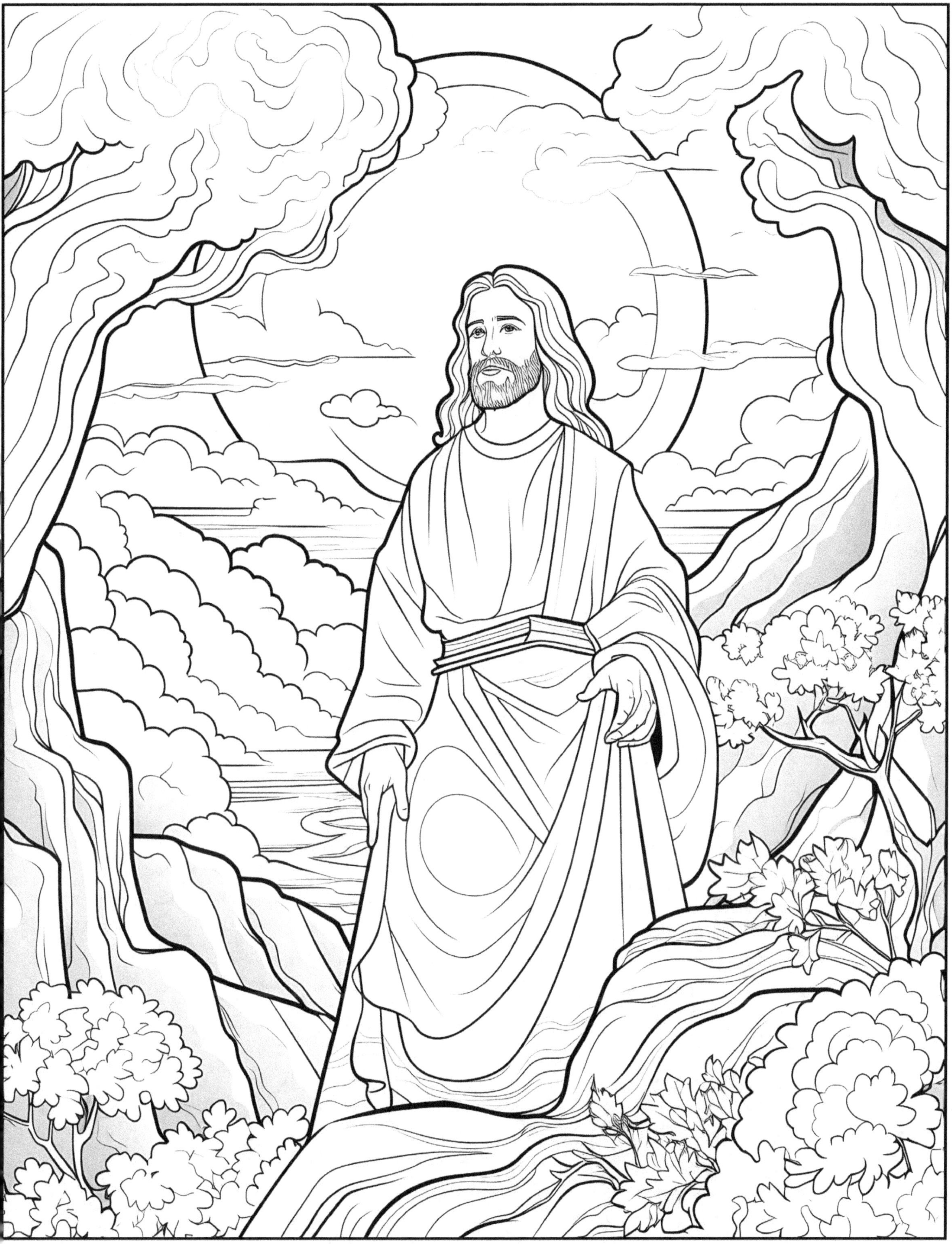

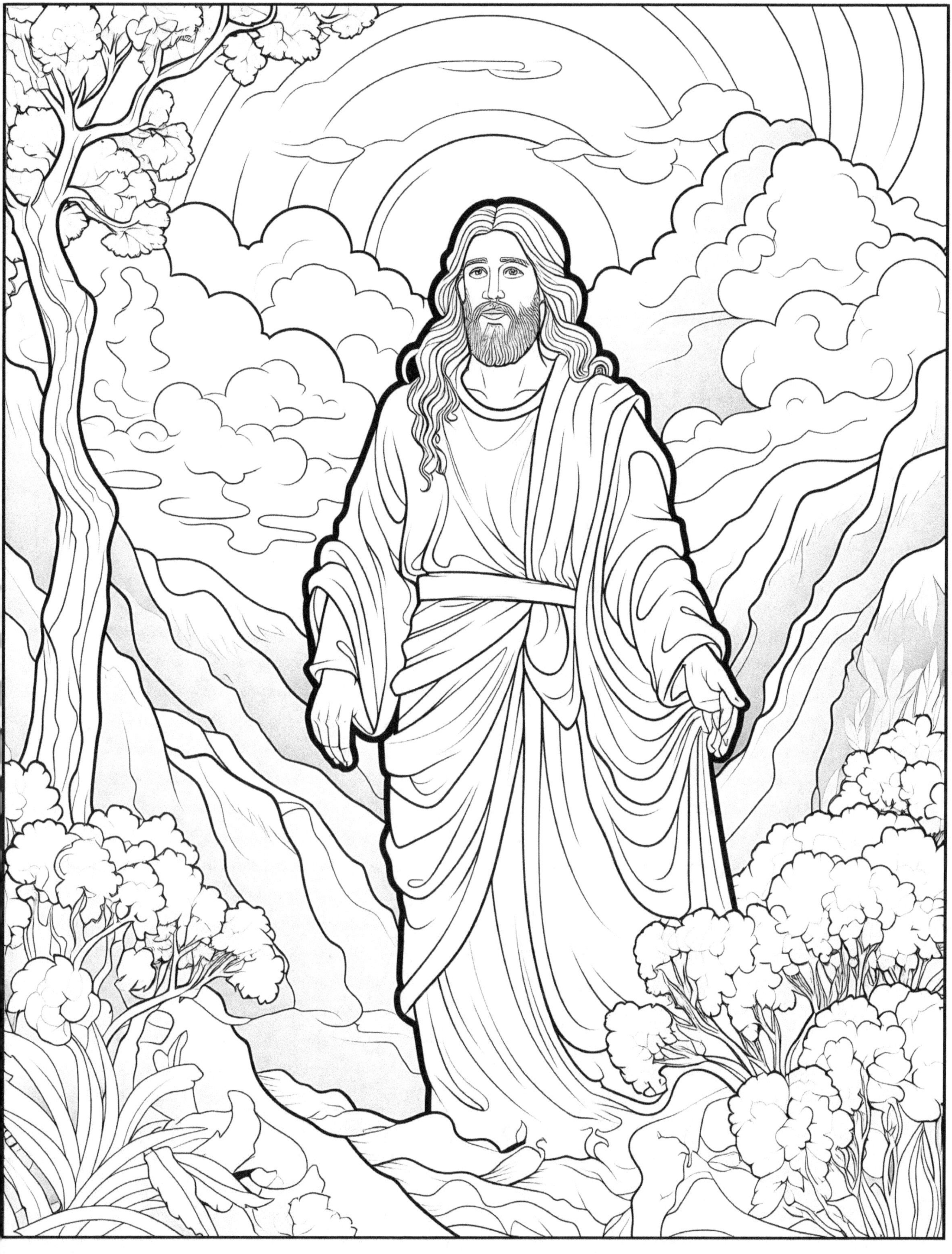

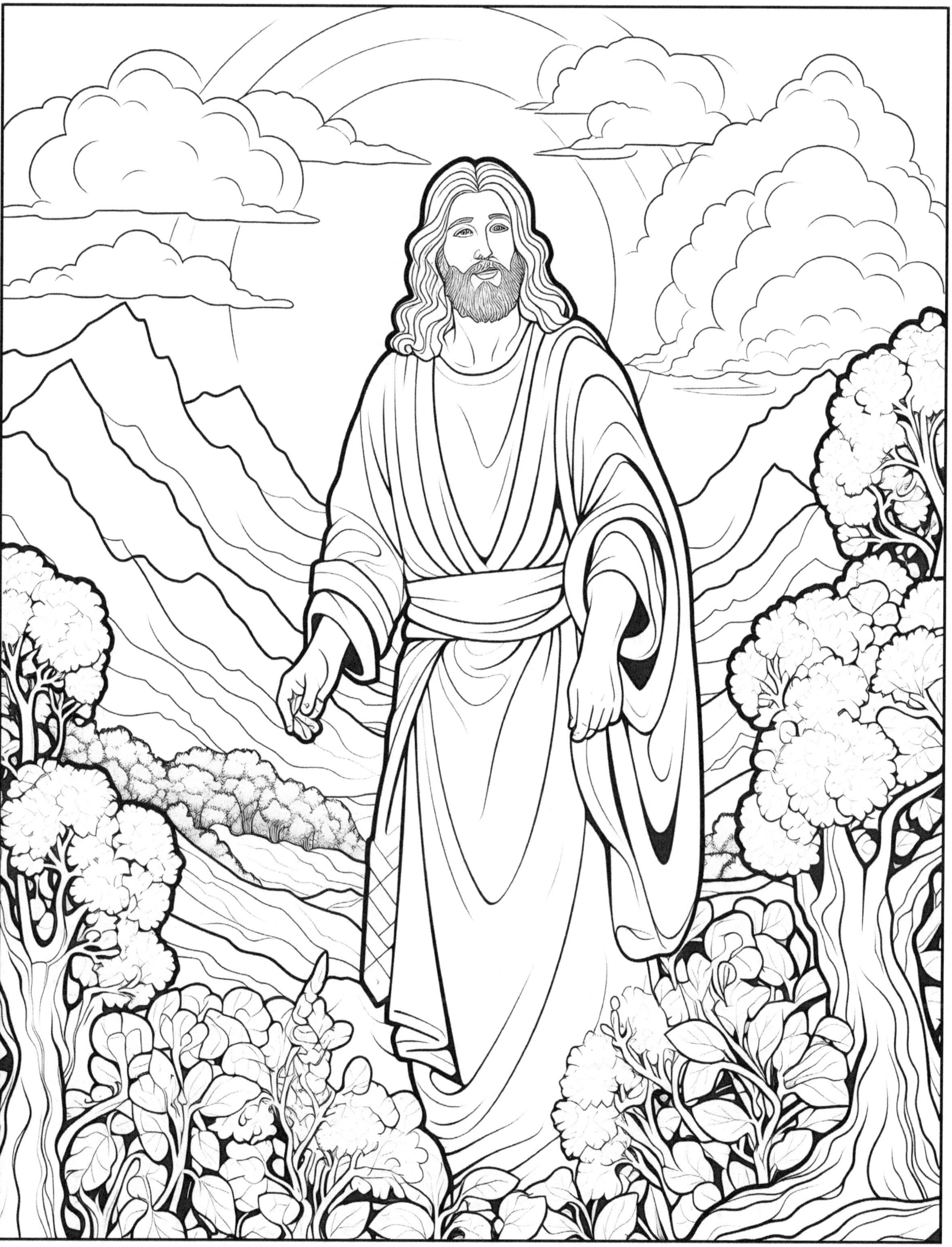

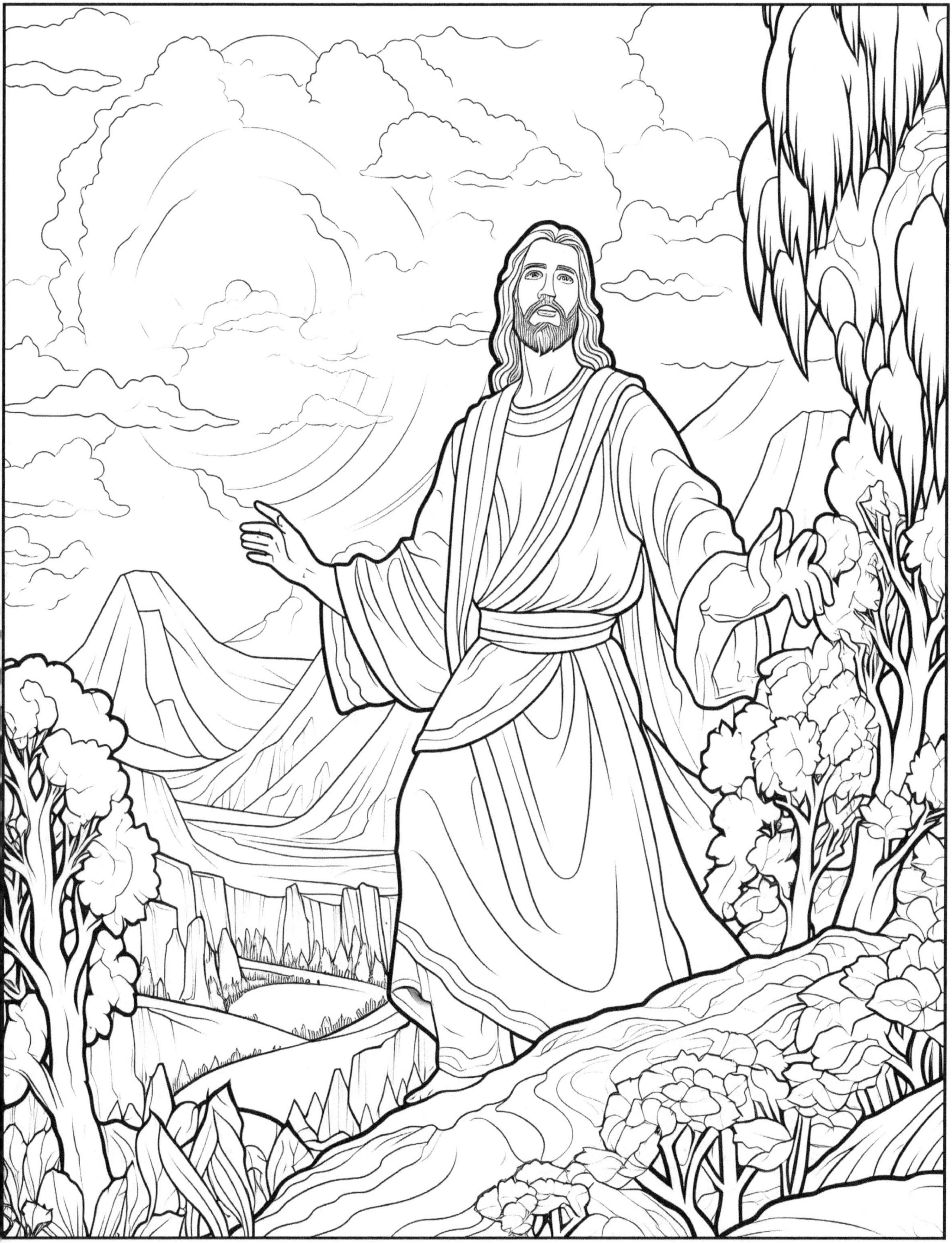

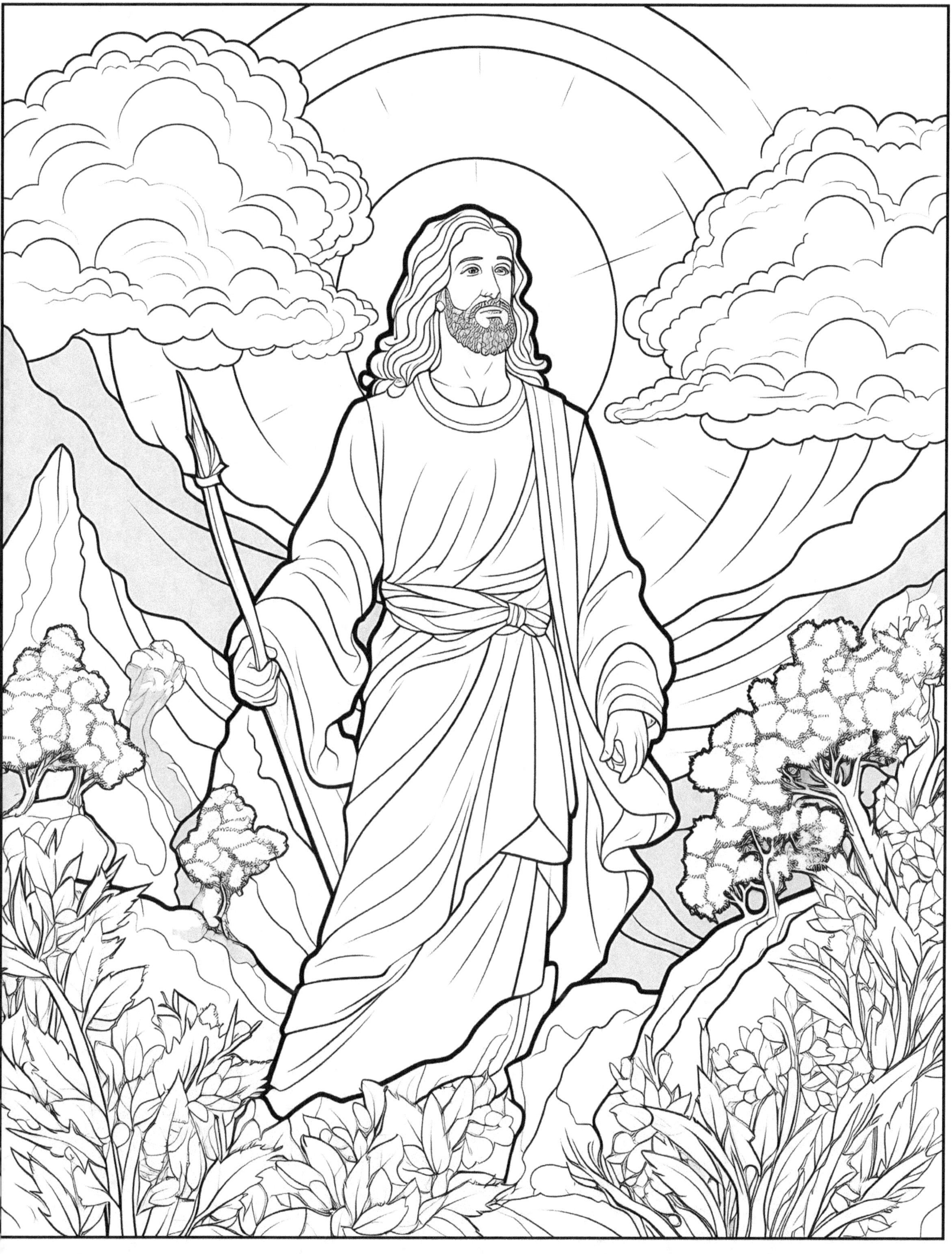

Grazie per aver acquistato il mio prodotto e aver contribuito alla creatività.

Akab Publisher

www.ingramcontent.com/pod-product-compliance
Lightning Source LLC
Chambersburg PA
CBHW082151290526
45794CB00008B/3250
* 9 7 9 8 8 6 1 5 3 6 6 1 5 *